The
Gay Agenda
2012

All Out

Juan Ahonen-Jover, Ph.D.

Published by **create**space

Third Edition

Book website: www.GayAgenda2012.com

Copyright © 2012 Juan Ahonen-Jover

All rights reserved.

Paperback ISBN-10:1479219401
Paperback ISBN-13: 978-1479219407

iBook ISBN-10: 0988328607
iBook ISBN-13: 978-0-9883286-0-0

Also available for Kindle

Dedication

This book is for all persons who
believe in the equality expressed in the
United States Declaration of Independence

"We hold these truths to be self-evident, that all men are created equal"

and in the United States Constitution:

"Nor deny to any person within its jurisdiction the equal protection of the laws."

Is This Book for *You?*

- If you are a heterosexual seeking to understand the most important social issue of our generation, this book is for you (especially Part I and Epilogue).

- If you are a parent or grandparent interested in family values and protecting your children, this book is for you (especially Parts I, II and Epilogue).

- If you are a policy maker, whether conservative or liberal, who wants to write laws that are fair, this book is for you (read it all).

- If you are a religious person and want to preserve your freedom of religion, this book is for you (especially Part I and Epilogue).

- If you are concerned about changes in society, including the redefinition of marriage, this book is for you (especially Parts I, II and Epilogue).

- If your sexual orientation or gender identity or expression does not fit the norm of the majority, this book is for you. You may know much of the information presented, but you will gain insights and inspiration for fighting for equal treatment under the law (so read it all and *take action*).

- If you are a believer in equality, this book is for you. You may know some of the book's content, but read it all and *take action.*

Contents

Preface

This book describes the Gay Agenda for 2012 in detail—what it is, and how and why lesbian, gay, bisexual, and transgender people and others want to change the United States (and the world).

Today in the United States, the core beliefs of the country are under attack. The freedom of religion is under attack. Family values are under attack. Individualism and the pursuit of happiness are under attack. The courts are under attack.

This book is about freedom, including the freedom of religion and the freedom to be yourself.

This book is also about our constitution and about one of our most cherished rights: to be treated equally under the law.

What would it be like if we could return to the vision of our great constitution?

What legislation would need to be added or modified to reach equal treatment under the law? How do we go about doing it?

This book shows a path to it, and it is an urgent *All Out* call for action.

Part I:

What Is LGBT?

1.

Who Are These Lesbian, Gay, Bisexual, and Transgender People (LGBT)?

They are your neighbors, your coworkers, your elected officials (even if you may not realize it), your children or grandchildren (even if they do not know it yet). They are a small part of the population, but they are everywhere—in every culture, religion, location, and profession. Some live as couples, some as singles, and some are married to somebody of the opposite gender. But what they all have in common is that their sexual orientation or gender identity or expression is different from the majority.

Some are exclusively attracted to members of the same gender. Others are attracted to both genders. Others feel that their anatomical gender of birth does not correspond to the gender their minds tell them they belong to. We call these people LGBT as the abbreviation for lesbian, gay, bisexual, and transgender.

Other people prefer to call themselves *queer*, which is an all-encompassing term for anybody who does not want to be classified as heterosexual or gay or lesbian or bisexual or transgender or any of the other classifications that are commonly in use. So, sometimes the term LGBTQ is also used to include *queer*. Also, the Q in LGBTQ can mean questioning, for people who are questioning their sexual orientation.

There is also the term *Two Spirits*, used by Native Americans. Several books have been written on the topic.

There are also people who are intersex, meaning that from birth they have both male and female genital characteristics.

Here is another, more recent term: *metrosexual*. It describes mostly men who are hip, cool, and fashionable. They are very comfortable with people of different sexual orientations and gender identities. Metrosexuals themselves can be of any sexual orientation or gender identity or expression, although most are heterosexual.

By now, you may think that this book is *not* for you—that it is all about a bunch of perverts and kinky stuff, all forbidden in the Bible. Please continue reading—this book really *is* for you, since it addresses some key questions:

- Why can't everybody just get along, marry somebody of the opposite sex, have children, and be a productive member of society?

- What type of a country are we building in the United States if we allow the collapse of the traditional family?

- What type of a country are we building if we abandon our bedrock principles of individuality, respect for religion, separation of religion from state, and separation of powers in the three government branches?

This book answers these important questions.

To have an opinion is easy. To learn the facts and be open to modifying our opinion based on new information is harder.

If you are not willing to even consider other points of view that in reality are closer to your opinions than you may think, then stop reading and give this book away.

Let's start with some fundamentals.

The Gay Agenda is not only about lesbian, gay, bisexual, and transgender people (LGBT). It is about *every single person,* because each of us has a sexual orientation and a gender identity and expression. As uncomfortable as the topic may be to some people, it is a very important component of who we are as people.

The American Psychological Association (www.apa.org/helpcenter/sexual-orientation.aspx) defines sexual orientation as follows:

> Sexual orientation refers to an enduring pattern of emotional, romantic, and/or sexual attractions to

men, women, or both sexes. Sexual orientation also refers to a person's sense of identity based on those attractions, related behaviors, and membership in a community of others who share those attractions.

Notice that sexual orientation refers to heterosexuality, homosexuality, and bisexuality. So laws and rules that apply to sexual orientation protects *every* person, *including heterosexuals.*

The other component to consider is gender identity and expression, which is defined by the American Psychological Association (www.apa.org/topics/sexuality/transgender.aspx) as follows:

Gender identity refers to a person's internal sense of being male, female, or something else; gender expression refers to the way a person communicates gender identity to others through behavior, clothing, hairstyles, voice, or body characteristics.

Again, gender identity is something that affects every person. Most people feel comfortable that their gender at birth matches the gender that they feel they belong to. But some people feel differently. Some like to cross-dress, which is independent of sexual orientation (in fact, most cross-dressers are heterosexual—many in happy marriages). Others feel that they need to change their gender to the one they feel is their true gender.

Note that sexual orientation (the people you are attracted to) is different from gender identity (the gender you belong to in your mind) and different from the expression of that gender. For instance, a male may have surgery to become a female (her gender identity is female), but at the same time be attracted to males (so her sexual orientation is heterosexual). Or you may be a heterosexual female who dresses more manly, so the gender expression may be that of a man—despite that you are a heterosexual female. All the potential combinations can be mind-boggling the first time you hear about it, but life is complex and not just black and white.

For whatever reason, many people in our society cannot comprehend why transgender people need to change the gender of birth. It is a sad reflection on our American society, one traditionally committed to freedom and happiness, that so many people do not respect others' freedom, especially about private personal matters such as contraception, sexual orientation, and gender identity and expression.

Before we proceed with the rest of the book, it is very important to understand that people who are gay or lesbian or bisexual or transgender are not weirdos. In fact many of them have made very important contributions to society. Appendix 1 lists many of them. The next chapter talks about everyday life.

2.

A Day in the Life of a Family

The alarm goes off. It is 6:00 a.m. It seems that the alarm always goes off too early.

Lisa drags herself out of bed. She barely makes it to the kitchen, where the coffee is already brewing. Ah! What technology can do! You set it up the night before, and coffee is ready when you wake up.

Thanks to the coffee, Lisa makes it to the shower, then wakes up the kids and prepares breakfast.

Mornings are always such a struggle. Rush, rush, and rush. It is not easy with four children. Lisa takes the kids to the school bus. Today is going to be a tough day. Katie, one of the couple's children, is home with the flu.

It is never easy with four children: Michael, Danielle, David, and Katie. The couple adopted each of them. Nobody wanted these children because they all have special needs: drug exposure during pregnancy, or HIV exposure in the womb, or development delays. They are great kids, but, through no fault of their own, they were rejected by other adoptive parents. Fortunately, the two kids who were exposed to HIV in the womb have tested negative. Things are going well.

The rest of the morning flies by with going to the supermarket, taking care of Katie, and doing three loads of laundry.

In the afternoon, Lisa takes the kids to after-school activities. Lisa is a very busy stay-at-home mom. She teaches the first communion classes in her church. She is also the volunteer coordinator for her children's elementary school. And she also started two Girl Scout troops.

She is the supermom that even teenagers are proud of.

Lisa rushes home to prepare dinner. Just after 7:00 p.m., Janice, her partner of eighteen years, gets home. She is exhausted after a full day of work as a manager of a state child welfare program. She is well respected for her work and knowledge (with a master's in public administration and a master's in social work).

The conversation at the dinner table centers on the children. It always does. Lisa and Janice ask them how was their day at school, review their homework, and so on—the usual stuff.

By midnight, they both have fallen sleep on the couch, pretending to watch TV.

They feel blessed for what they have. Tomorrow surely the alarm will go off again at 6:00 a.m.

For these two moms, life is not very different from any other family with children.

Or so they thought.

3.

A Bad Day in the Life of a Family

Lisa and Janice—along with their three youngest adopted children Danielle, David, and Katie—flew from rainy western Washington to Florida one sunny day in February 2007. The family could not wait to board a gay family cruise to the Bahamas. The family was there to celebrate the couple's anniversary and in David's words "meet other kids with two moms or two dads."

This was a trip that the children (and their parents) had so much looked forward to! They were in line early to board the ship. They had lunch together just after 1 p.m. Everyone was excited about relaxing together for an entire week as a family. What a great adventure awaited them!

After lunch, the children asked impatiently to explore the ship and headed to the top deck where they found a basketball court. A court on a cruise ship! What could be more cool?

Janice said she was going to unpack and take a siesta (nothing like taking on a Latin tradition while in Miami). The ship wasn't scheduled to depart until 3:00 p.m., so there was plenty of time before the sail-away party.

Lisa, never one to sit still, joined the children on the top deck with her coffee in one hand and a camera in the other. Not different from what any mother would do. It is such a happy day!

While taking pictures of the children, Lisa suddenly collapsed on the basketball court spilling her coffee and dropping the camera. The children just 9 years to 12 years old helped pick up their mom and navigated their way down ten decks to find their cabin to bang on the door and wake-up their other mom, Janice.

With the help of Janice they flagged down a porter to get a wheelchair since Lisa was unable to stand on her own. The family headed immediately to the medical center onboard. The doctor established that Lisa was gravelly ill. He then requested the ship's captain to delay departure and ordered an urgent transfer to the trauma center in Miami at Jackson Memorial Hospital. Medics arrived to take over emergency care of Lisa while a sheriff's deputy escorted Janice, the children and their luggage to a waiting taxi. The taxi and medics carrying Lisa arrived at Ryder Trauma Center almost simultaneously around three-thirty in the afternoon.

Janice attempted to follow the gurney carrying Lisa through the emergency entrance but was asked to go to the waiting room and speak with the clerk. Janice settled the children in some chairs and headed to the desk to speak with a clerk. She asked to fill out admitting papers for Lisa, her partner, but was told to "take a seat" and wait for someone to come speak with her.

Not quite forty minutes later, a man appeared and introduced himself as Garnett Frederick, a hospital social worker. He then informed Janice that she and her family were in an "antigay city and state," and that if Janice wanted to find out about Lisa's condition or even see her, she needed a healthcare proxy. He turned to leave but Janice immediately asked for his fax number and informed him that he would get the documents.

Do you know of any couple who travels with a healthcare proxy? If Janice and Lisa were a man and a woman, would anybody have asked for any documents? Would anybody have to ask, even if the couple were not married, to be allowed in the room with each other?

Janice and Lisa had their healthcare power of attorney, living wills and advanced directives documents drawn up in 2001 shortly after Janice was diagnosed with multiple sclerosis on the advice couple's adoption attorney. They tucked the documents away never envisioning they would need them until they were much older. On that day, Lisa was only 39 years old. Janice, a trained trauma and emergency department social worker, ensured that the couple kept their healthcare proxy and decision making documents up to date.

Janice wondered in that moment at Ryder Trauma center why their love and commitment of eighteen years was not recognized. Nevertheless, she jumped into action and called a trusted friend, who rushed to the couple's house and faxed the decision making documents to Ryder Trauma center and called Janice just after

4:20 p.m. that the fax was received at the hospital only forty-five minutes after Lisa's arrival from the ship.

All of Janice's pleas to find out Lisa's condition or to speak to medical personnel went unanswered by a seemingly uncaring desk clerk. Janice watched as other families, some with young children, were escorted back through locked doors to see their loved ones. Yet Janice and their children anguish increased with every minute that passed.

With papers in hand, one would think that even in an antigay city and state, Janice would be informed of Lisa's medical condition. At 6 p.m.—two and half hours after their arrival—Janice was faced with a decision that would change their family forever. Surgeons informed Janice that Lisa was nearly brain dead and they needed to know if they should proceed with surgery. Even if Lisa survived the surgery, she would live in a persistent vegetative state. Janice was forced to make the decision to follow Lisa's wishes of donating her organs without even seeing her. After the surgeons left, Janice was alone to tell the children that the other mom was going to Heaven.

Over the next five and a half hours, Janice begged and pleaded to see Lisa and bring their children to the room to say goodbye. Janice resorted to showing the children's birth certificates, which listed both of them as mothers, to the desk clerk in an attempt to establish that the children where in fact Lisa's children. They were still not allowed to see their mother.

Janice requested a catholic priest to administer Lisa's last rites. It was only then that she was given one opportunity to see Lisa for only five minutes

After 11:30 p.m., when Janice and the children had waited eight hours in the hospital waiting room, Lisa's sister arrived after driving from her home in Jacksonville, Florida. Janice led Lisa's sister inside and brought her to the same desk clerk who worked there all night. Lisa's sister simply stated, "I'm Lisa Pond's sister and I am here to see her." She was informed that Lisa was moved an hour earlier to the neuro ICU and was given the room number. Lisa's sister was not asked for identification or any paperwork proving her family relationship.

Lisa Pond died of a brain aneurysm at age thirty-nine on February 19, 2007, in Jackson Memorial Hospital. Her children and the love of her life, Janice Langbehn, were a few feet away—but in another room without being able to be with Lisa in her final moments. Without being able to touch her. Without being able to kiss her good-bye. Without being able to say "I love you" for the final time.

This is a true story. All the information is factual. That this cruel story happened in Miami, a city that has prospered from gay tourism, tells you that it can happen anywhere.

Janice Langbehn sued the hospital. The judge dismissed the case, stating that despite that the hospital "exhibited a lack of compassion and was unbecoming of a renowned trauma center like Ryder [Jackson Memorial Hospital Trauma Center]. Unfortunately, no relief is available for these failures based on the allegations pleaded in the amended complaint."

In other words, there is nothing to sue about, because there is no law that had been broken. Hospital visitation discrimination like this was allowed in Florida and other states until January 18, 2011, when new regulations took into effect at the urging of President Obama after learning of the Langbehn-Pond story.

Lisa and Janice, together for eighteen years, parents of four children that nobody else wanted, were cruelly denied a most basic human need: to have your loved ones next to you when you die. In Janice's words "Holding Lisa's hand is not a *gay* right but a *human* right."

4.

Your Family's Values

Family is very personal, and how you raise your family is up to you.

But as a father and mother said: *"I don't want others to impose their family values on my family."*

It is all about *your family's* values. For example, this father and mother's family values are clear: they have two daughters—one lesbian, the other one non-lesbian. Taking turns, they both said, "Our family's values are that we treat our two daughters the same. We teach them the same things. We want them to have the same opportunities. We want them to be happy in their lives and one day to marry someone they love and start their own families. We treat our two daughters equally and want the government to do the same. These are our family's values."

One day recently, this family found out that they held a prejudice that they had not previously realized. They encouraged their non-lesbian daughter to bring her boyfriend home for dinner (but not stay overnight) to ensure that he could get to know the family and vice versa. However, they were uncomfortable asking the lesbian daughter to bring her girlfriend.

The parents said: "We did not realize that we were treating our two daughters differently and that we could cause harm that way. Now we check everything we do as parents, to show both our daughters that we love them equally and unconditionally. And it is fine for our daughter to bring her girlfriend for dinner and family outings—but neither of our daughters get to bring a boyfriend or girlfriend overnight!" Parents and daughters all laughed together as they recounted the story.

What this father and mother are doing is in fact very good parenting. Scientific research by the Family Acceptance Project of San Francisco State University (familyproject.sfsu.edu) shows the following:

- Suicide attempts by LGBT youth who have high rejection from the family are more than *eight times* the attempts in families with low rejection for their LGBT children.

- Illegal drug use by LGBT youth who experience high rejection from their family is more than *three times* the use for those in families with low rejection for their LGBT children.

- Similarly, the risk of HIV infection is more than *three times* the risk LGBT children in families with a high rejection for them.

- Yet another interesting statistic: 92 percent of LGBT youth in a family that is highly accepting believe that they can be a happy LGBT adult, while only 35 percent of those in a family that is not accepting believe it so.

Several religious leaders are working with the Family Acceptance Project because these scientific findings have opened their minds that tough love can be very detrimental to the health (and survival) of young LGBT people.

Each family member is entitled to his or her faith. You may believe that LGBT people will not go to Heaven. Other family members may believe in an all-loving God, and that a good person (whether gay or non-gay) will go to Heaven. But independently of your faith, every good parent knows that *love for a child must be unconditional*, in good times and in bad.

There are, however, several parental behaviors that increase the risk of LGBT children developing health and mental problems. These parental behaviors are determined to be unhealthy based not on opinion but on scientific research by the Family Acceptance Project (familyproject.sfsu.edu). Here are nine behaviors to avoid:

1. "Hitting, slapping or physically hurting your child because of their LGBT identity."

2. "Verbal harassment or name-calling because of your child's LGBT identity."

3. "Excluding LGBT youth from family and family identity."

4. "Blocking access to LGBT friends, events and resources."

5. "Blaming your child when they are discriminated against because of their LGBT identity."

6. "Pressuring your child to be more (or less) masculine or feminine."

7. "Telling your children that God will punish them because they are gay."

8. "Telling your child that you are ashamed of them or that how they look or act will shame the family."

9. "Making your child keep their LGBT identity a secret in the family and not letting them talk about it."

You determine your family's values. All parents want the best for their children. When parents decide what's best for their children, they draw on experiences with their parents (good or bad), and all the other experiences they've learned over their lives. But most parents have no experience dealing with LGBT children. Fortunately, research conducted by the Family Acceptance Project shows parental behaviors that can be most helpful to their LGBT children. These recommendations are not based on opinions or beliefs but on research. Here are eleven things to do:

1. "Talk with your child or foster child about their LGBT identity."

2. "Express affection when your child tells you or when you learn that your child is gay or transgender."

3. "Support your child's LGBT identity even though you may feel uncomfortable."

4. "Advocate for your child when he or she is mistreated because of their LGBT identity."

5. "Require that other family members respect your LGBT child."

6. "Bring your child to LGBT organizations or events."

7. "Talk with your clergy and help your faith community to support LGBT people."

8. "Connect your child with an LGBT adult role model to show them options for the future."

9. "Welcome your child's LGBT friends and partners to your home."

10. "Support your child's gender expression."

11. "Believe your child can have a happy future as an LGBT adult."

This science is opening up many minds—teaching parents to understand the unintended consequences of their past behavior.

For religious parents this may appear like a conflict, especially when some churches say that homosexuality is an abomination. But more and more religious leaders are reaching out after seeing the science—and more and more Christian parents accept what Jesus has always taught: unconditional love and commitment. Not tough love. But *unconditional love and commitment*, which is the basis of marriage and of having children—good parents want to protect their child from harm.

The father and mother in this story concluded by saying,

> In our family we do not value treating one child differently from the other. We value, cherish, and celebrate their uniqueness. Because each of our children is a gift.

So, you determine your family's values.

But what's the definition of a family?

5.

Defining *Family*

In the last few chapters we have met two families. First, we encountered the Langbehn-Pond family. A family, consecrated in a holy union by their church on October 12, 1991, that found itself tragically discriminated while in Miami in 2007, despite that LGBT tourists and residents are an important part of the economy. They were so discriminated that Lisa Pond was left to die alone despite her spouse and children being in a nearby room.

The second family we encountered was very traditional: a husband and wife with two daughters. Their family's values are to ensure that both of their daughters are treated the same even if they have different sexual orientations. This family, like so many others, does not accept that others tell them what their family's values should be.

But how *does* one define a family? Traditionalists have a clear answer: mother + father + children. This is *their* definition of family. What's *your* definition?

For example, here is the definition that the Baptist Health South Florida has for a family (in their 2011 *Outcomes*—a compilation of articles from their Center for Performance Excellence):

> The word *family* triggers images of different "support groups" for each of us. Over time, the "social support group" to us changes, shifts, or expands throughout our lives.
>
> At Baptist Health, each patient defines those individuals who are most important to them—who they view as "family." We recognize and value the importance of these individuals in the healing process. These people may include, but are not limited to, family, friends, and/or other support persons, such as a spouse, a domestic partner (including same-sex domestic partner), other

relatives, neighbors, co-workers or clergy. **In other words, each patient has the right to define who can be present and participate in their care and visitation.**

The bold typeface is in the original article. Note that Baptist Health South Florida is a *faith-based* healthcare organization ranking at the top in the United States. They understand the definition of a family, since they see patients constantly defining who their families are.

Each of us knows who our true family is: the people we turn to when we are most in need.

How have we come to allow others to impose who should be our family?

This is an attack on our personal freedom.

People use several arguments to deny others' freedoms. Let's examine these arguments one by one in the next chapter.

6.

It's Unnatural!

Some people think that homosexual, bisexual, and transgender people are mentally sick, that what they do is unnatural, and that the Bible says that it is an abomination. These beliefs serve as a justification for people to discriminate, such as to deny a family the right to be together when the mother is dying at a public hospital.

Would God accept the behavior of people in that hospital in Miami that would not allow Lisa's partner to be next to her as she was dying? What about the children, who had nothing to do with their parents' sexual orientation?

Let's discus now one of the most common arguments used to discriminate.

HOMOSEXUALITY IS A SIN AGAINST NATURE

To see if it is a sin against nature, we need to check whether homosexuality and bisexuality exist in animals in nature.

Evidence is very clear that many animals exhibit homosexual and bisexual behaviors. Here are just a few examples from Wikipedia (en.wikipedia.org/wiki/Homosexual_behavior_in_animals):

- **Giraffes:** about nine out of ten matings occur between males.
- **Domesticated sheep:** about 10 percent of males do not mate females, but only males.
- **Black swans:** about 25 percent of the matings are between males. Male couples also raise young black swans.
- **Western gulls:** 10 to 15 percent of females show homosexual behavior.
- **Wild ducks:** about 19 percent of all pairings are male with male.

- **Penguins:** many male-to-male long term relationships reported in zoos, including building nests together.
- **Vultures:** bisexual vultures have been documented in zoos.
- **Pigeons:** documented male-male and female-female relationships. Same-gender couples build nests together.
- **American bison:** same-sex relationships are documented as common.
- **Bonobos (apes):** considered a bisexual species (60 percent of sexual activity is between two or more females).
- **Dolphins:** well-documented bisexual behavior, especially among bottlenose dolphins.
- **Elephants:** well-documented bisexual behavior, with stronger bonds between males.
- **Japanese Macaque (monkey):** both male-male and female-female relationships.
- **Lions:** about 8 percent of mountings are male-male.
- **Spotted hyena:** strong female-to-female relationships.
- **Lizards:** female lizards can take masculine or feminine sexual roles.
- **Dragonflies:** high incidence of mating among males.

This article also states, "No species has been found in which homosexual behavior has not been shown to exist, with the exception of species that never have sex at all." Let's agree that we cannot say that homosexuality and bisexuality are unnatural when it has been well documented in nature.

Some people would say, "Fine, we cannot say that it is unnatural, but these people are mentally sick." The next chapter responds to this pronouncement.

7.

You Are Sick!

Given the scientific evidence, we need to agree that homosexuality and bisexuality occur naturally in animals. What about in humans? Has this topic been studied by science? The answer is yes. Research by psychologists like Alfred Kinsey, Magnus Hirschfeld, and Sigmund Freud, among others, shows that sexual orientation appears as a spectrum from totally heterosexual, to bisexual, to totally homosexual.

Repeated studies show that people fall into different parts of the spectrum of sexual orientation. And this is a very natural phenomenon. Similarly, handedness falls into a continuous spectrum: most people are right-handed, some are left-handed, and some are ambidextrous.

The American Psychological Association (www.apa.org/helpcenter/sexual-orientation.aspx) confirms:

> Both heterosexual behavior and homosexual behavior are normal aspects of human sexuality. Both have been documented in many different cultures and historical eras. Despite the persistence of stereotypes that portray lesbian, gay, and bisexual people as disturbed, several decades of research and clinical experience have led all mainstream medical and mental health organizations in this country to conclude that these orientations represent normal forms of human experience. Lesbian, gay, and bisexual relationships are normal forms of human bonding. Therefore, these mainstream organizations long ago abandoned classifications of homosexuality as a mental disorder.

Clearly, scientific organizations have concluded that homosexuality, heterosexuality, and bisexuality are normal forms of the human experience and that they are not mental disorders.

So we cannot say that homosexuality is unnatural since it occurs in nature; we cannot say that people with a homosexual sexual orientation are sick since it has been proven scientifically not to be the case.

But, you may say, the Bible says homosexuality is an abomination. You are right on this one—read on.

8.

The Bible Says So

We have already seen that we cannot call homosexuality unnatural, since it is well documented that it happens in nature.

Nor can we say that homosexuality is a disease, since the American Psychological Association and other organizations have clearly said that it is a normal aspect of human sexuality.

So, it's not unnatural and it is not a disease. However, some people believe that, based on what the Bible says, homosexuality is an abomination.

Indeed, Leviticus 18:22 (King James Version) clearly says, "Thou shalt not lie with mankind, as with womankind: it is an abomination." Some experts contend that the term *abomination* is mistranslated. But since religion is based on personal faith, we should respect those who take the meaning literally.

Furthermore, Leviticus 20:13 (King James Version) establishes the death penalty for homosexual acts:

> If a man also lie with mankind, as he lieth with a woman, both of them have committed an abomination: they shall surely be put to death; their blood shall be upon them.

But if you are willing to accept that homosexual acts are an abomination subject to the death penalty, then you have to accept the penalty that the same chapter of Leviticus 20 establishes:

> **Leviticus 20:9:** For every one that curseth his father or his mother shall be surely put to death: he hath cursed his father or his mother; his blood shall be upon him.

> **Leviticus 20:10:** And the man that committeth adultery with another man's wife, even he that

committeth adultery with his neighbour's wife, the adulterer and the adulteress shall surely be put to death.

Leviticus 20:11: And the man that lieth with his father's wife hath uncovered his father's nakedness: both of them shall surely be put to death; their blood shall be upon them.

Leviticus 20:12: And if a man lie with his daughter in law, both of them shall surely be put to death: they have wrought confusion; their blood shall be upon them.

Leviticus 20:13: If a man also lie with mankind, as he lieth with a woman, both of them have committed an abomination: they shall surely be put to death; their blood shall be upon them.

Leviticus 20:14: And if a man take a wife and her mother, it is wickedness: they shall be burnt with fire, both he and they; that there be no wickedness among you.

Leviticus 20:15: And if a man lie with a beast, he shall surely be put to death: and ye shall slay the beast.

Leviticus 20:16: And if a woman approach unto any beast, and lie down thereto, thou shalt kill the woman, and the beast: they shall surely be put to death; their blood shall be upon them.

Leviticus 20:17: And if a man shall take his sister, his father's daughter, or his mother's daughter, and see her nakedness, and she see his nakedness; it is a wicked thing; and they shall be cut off in the sight of their people: he hath uncovered his sister's nakedness; he shall bear his iniquity.

Leviticus 20:18: And if a man shall lie with a woman having her sickness, and shall uncover her nakedness; he hath discovered her fountain, and she hath uncovered the fountain of her blood: and both of them shall be cut off from among their people.

> **Leviticus 20:19:** And thou shalt not uncover the nakedness of thy mother's sister, nor of thy father's sister: for he uncovereth his near kin: they shall bear their iniquity.

> **Leviticus 20:20:** And if a man shall lie with his uncle's wife, he hath uncovered his uncle's nakedness: they shall bear their sin; they shall die childless.

> **Leviticus 20:21:** And if a man shall take his brother's wife, it is an unclean thing: he hath uncovered his brother's nakedness; they shall be childless.

So, if you curse your father or mother, you should be put to death. And if you commit adultery with a married woman, both of you should be put to death. So if you accept that homosexual acts are an abomination that deserves to be put to death, then you should be consistent with the other commandments in the same chapter of Leviticus. But to be really consistent, you should also adhere to other commandments in Leviticus:

> **Leviticus 11:10–12:** And all that have not fins and scales in the seas, and in the rivers, of all that move in the waters, and of any living thing which is in the waters, they shall be an abomination unto you. They shall be even an abomination unto you; ye shall not eat of their flesh, but ye shall have their carcasses in abomination. Whatsoever hath no fins nor scales in the waters, that shall be an abomination unto you.

So, not only homosexual acts are an abomination, but eating shrimp and other fishes without fins is an abomination too. The point is not to debate or contest *your* interpretation of the Bible. Some Christians believe that the translation may not consider the context of the times and the exact meaning of the words. Other Christians believe that the Bible should be read literally; if this is your belief, please act consistently by choosing what you cannot eat and lobby to establish the death penalty, not only for homosexual acts but also for the heterosexual acts listed in Leviticus. The point here is not to change your religious beliefs, but to encourage you to be *consistent*. In fact, it is very important to respect and protect the freedom of religion, as the next chapter attests.

9.

Your Freedom of Religion

Clearly, in a civilized society, we are not going to execute men who commit adultery with married women, just as we are not going to execute people who commit homosexual acts. Similarly, in a civilized society, we are not going to call people with a homosexual sexual orientation an abomination but remain silent about people who commit the abomination, per Leviticus 11, of eating shrimp, lobster, clams, mussels, or any shellfish.

Whether you believe or not that the U.S. Constitution requires separation of church and state, there is no debate that every American wants to respect each other's freedom of religion. It is true: some religions do believe that homosexual acts should be penalized and that indeed people with a homosexual sexual orientation should not be treated equally under the law. But some other religions differ. They believe that every person is a child of God, loved by God, and should be treated equally.

So, which freedom of religion do we protect?

We should protect the freedom of each religion, since we can only protect your freedom of religion if we protect other's freedom of religion. If your religion believes that homosexual acts are an abomination and does not allow people of the same gender to marry, it is fine. If your religion accepts people with a homosexual sexual orientation and their right to marry, fine too. Government should not impose on any religion whom to marry (or divorce). Or force any religion to have bishops who are homosexual or female.

Government cannot impose one religion's views on another. This is why each religion is regulated by its own laws; and civic life by its own laws. We all share in common the United States Declaration of Independence that states:

> We hold these truths to be self-evident, that all men are created equal.

And in the United States Constitution:

> Nor deny to any person within its jurisdiction the equal protection of the laws.

The greatness of our country comes from not allowing Sharia law to control all of us. Nor do we allow Jewish law, or Catholic law, or Baptist law to control all of us. Every individual is free to follow the law of his or her church, while the government creates and enforces civil law.

Still, some people say that our *civil* laws should not treat people with a homosexual sexual orientation equally because homosexuality is a choice. But, is it a choice? The next chapter tackles this important question.

10.

Is Homosexuality a Choice?

Sexual orientation defines our attraction to other people. By definition, sexual orientation can be heterosexual (attracted to people of different gender), homosexual (attracted to people of the same gender) or bisexual (attracted to people of either gender).

So the question is, "Is sexual orientation a choice?"

Ask this question to yourself. Is *your* sexual orientation a choice? If you answer yes, when did you choose your sexual orientation? How did you make that choice?

Or, more pointedly, for heterosexuals: When did you decide to be a heterosexual? Could you decide you were heterosexual even before you had sex? Or did you always know because you were just born that way? Did it just come naturally?

Certainly, most readers have answered NO—meaning that sexual orientation was not a choice for them. Bisexual individuals may answer that at some point they were attracted to one gender, and at some other point in their life to the other, or that they were equally attracted to both.

If your child tells you that he or she is gay or lesbian or bisexual or transgender, do not blame yourself. *You did nothing wrong.* You did not influence him or her to be LGBT, nor did your parents influence you to be a heterosexual. Just as homosexual parents cannot influence their children to be LGBT. It is the way it is. There is growing research that the sexual orientation of the parents—heterosexual, homosexual, or bisexual—does not affect the orientation of the children they raise.

The people who believe that homosexuality is a choice use this to deny people with a different sexual orientation or gender identity equal protection under the law. They claim that the law should protect all citizens equally regardless of race, gender, or national origin because those factors are obviously not a choice.

But here is the catch: while the law protects against discrimination based on non-choice characteristics such as race, gender, and national origin, it also protects *religion*—which is clearly a personal choice. So you cannot fairly say that it is OK to discriminate against gays because being gay is a choice.

But there is yet another argument that some people still use to justify discrimination against gay, lesbian, bisexual, and transgender people. They say it can be cured! Let's consider this question in the next chapter.

11.

Let *Me* Straighten *You*

If your sexual orientation is heterosexual, do you think that with therapy you could become homosexual?

You are very likely to answer: *"No way. I do not want to change, and nobody would be able to make me homosexual, anyway."*

Similarly, most homosexuals do not want to change their sexual orientation.

However, there is heavy societal pressure to belong to the majority. So whether because of their religion, or their not knowing that sexual orientation falls into a spectrum, or fear of rejection by society, some people still struggle with their sexual orientation. They try to change their sexual orientation to heterosexual and "be cured." Some families, for similar reasons, bring their children to therapy (called reparative or conversion therapy) to make them straight.

But—as hard as it is to believe for those who think that homosexuality is an abomination (remember, eating shrimp is another abomination)—there is nothing to be cured.

The most important study on the subject was conducted in 2001 by Robert Spitzer, MD, a well-respected professor of psychiatry at Columbia University. Dr. Spitzer addressed the issue of whether individuals could change their sexual orientation from homosexual to heterosexual using reparative or conversation therapy. He concluded that *some* highly motivated individuals could do it. The report was published in the *Archives of Sexual Behavior,* but was not peer-reviewed, a critical requirement for any scientific work. Eventually, Dr. Spitzer concluded that his research was fundamentally flawed, and that there was no evidence that reparative therapy worked because statements from participants about their self-evaluation of the success of such therapy could not be relied upon.

This is what the American Psychological Association (www.apa.org/helpcenter/sexual-orientation.aspx) has to say about therapies to change sexual orientation:

> To date, there has been no scientifically adequate research to show that therapy aimed at changing sexual orientation (sometimes called reparative or conversion therapy) is safe or effective. Furthermore, it seems likely that the promotion of change therapies reinforces stereotypes and contributes to a negative climate for lesbian, gay, and bisexual persons. This appears to be especially likely for lesbian, gay, and bisexual individuals who grow up in more conservative religious settings.

So there is no evidence that such therapies are safe or effective!

The most prominent organization involved in so-called reparative or conversion therapy is Exodus International. In an interesting twist, Michael Bussee, one of its cofounders, left the organization in 1979 to live together with another cofounder of Exodus, Gary Cooper. To go even further, they had a commitment ceremony in 1982 (well before civil unions or marriage equality existed).

Years later, in October 2000, the Chairman of Exodus International, John Paulk, was removed from his position from the board after being spotted drinking and flirting at a gay bar in Washington, DC.

More recently, in 2011, John Smid, the former executive director of Love in Action (another organization that claimed to "straighten homosexuals"), said: "I never met a man who experienced a change from homosexual to heterosexual."

Putting a final nail to this coffin, Alan Chambers, the president of Exodus International, said in June 2012, that "there was no cure for homosexuality and that 'reparative therapy' offered false hopes to gays and could even be harmful."

So it doesn't work.

A very good resource and an organization worth supporting is Truth Wins Out (thruthwinsout.org). This organization specializes on debunking the ex-gay myth and counters disinformation campaigns about LGBT people. Its founder, Wayne Besen, is the author of *Anything but Straight: Unmasking the Scandals and Lies Behind the Ex-Gay Myth*. It is a book worth reading if you want to know more about this topic.

Some people may say, OK, I accept gays, but please do not flaunt it! This concern is addressed in the following chapter.

12.

Don't Flaunt It!

Some people say they can *tolerate* people who are gay, lesbian, bisexual, or transgender—but they add: just don't flaunt it! These people think that not "flaunting" sexual orientation, or hiding it, is a good compromise. In reality this so-called compromise is harming (albeit unintentionally) LGBT people.

An important part of a healthy mind is to be able to be who you are. This was a main argument expressed by the Chairman of the Joint Chiefs of Staff Admiral Mullen in support of the repeal of Don't Ask, Don't Tell: it is *immoral* to force people to lie and hide who they are.

Furthermore, a civilized society means that we accept other people —not just tolerate them. They are our equals. We try to understand other people, accept them and respect them. For instance, many years ago, the World Jewish Congress changed its vocabulary from "tolerance" to "respect."

It is wonderful to see a couple holding hands and showing their love. It is wonderful independently of the gender of the couple. Notice that I am talking about public displays of affection—not talking about having sex in public (which is not appropriate whether the couple is same-gender or different-gender).

But what about the children? Some people say, "I do not want my children to see a homosexual couple—it is bad for the child!" Some people say that out of concern that seeing such a couple will make the child homosexual. Of course, this is not true: If you are heterosexual, can you fathom for a second that you would have become homosexual just by seeing a same-gender couple holding hands when you were a child? Let's be real.

In fact, you may be causing harm to your children if they see you reacting negatively about a same-gender couple's public display of affection. The message that you are sending is that homosexuality is wrong and that you may not love your children if they are homosexual. Seeing a same-gender public display of affection is an opportunity for you to teach the importance of understanding, acceptance and respect for other human beings—and to let your children know that you will still love them even if they are homosexual or bisexual or transgender. Because you *will* still love them—won't you?

For those interested in the science, here is what the American Psychological Association has to say (www.apa.org/helpcenter/sexual-orientation.aspx)

> Sexual orientation is commonly discussed as if it were solely a characteristic of an individual, like biological sex, gender identity, or age. This perspective is incomplete because sexual orientation is defined in terms of relationships with others. People express their sexual orientation through behaviors with others, including such simple actions as holding hands or kissing. Thus, sexual orientation is closely tied to the intimate personal relationships that meet deeply felt needs for love, attachment, and intimacy. In addition to sexual behaviors, these bonds include nonsexual physical affection between partners, shared goals and values, mutual support, and ongoing commitment. Therefore, sexual orientation is not merely a personal characteristic within an individual. Rather, one's sexual orientation defines the group of people in which one is likely to find the satisfying and fulfilling romantic relationships that are an essential component of personal identity for many people.

So, it is about flaunting it. The freedom to be yourself is a part of one's sexual orientation and gender identity and expression, and is a necessary component of a healthy lifestyle. It is about the freedom and respect to be yourself. Some people get it—check the next chapter.

13.

Understand, Accept, and Respect

More than thirty years ago, a young man, proud of being the big man in high school, started his first day in college to discover that he had been assigned a gay roommate. He was surprised, but accepted it. After their freshman year, their lives took different courses. This young man ended up on Wall Street and was by the Twin Towers on September 11, 2001. Thankfully, he survived.

Life continued, and when President Obama announced his support for the freedom to marry, this young man e-mailed his freshman gay roommate of more than thirty years ago:

> With the President coming out and making a statement on same sex marriage I reference you often. I speak that you and I still stay in touch after all these years and that you were the first person to contact me after 9/11. I will always remember that. I have you and your friends to thank for enabling me to understand, accept and respect gay people. Being 18 and big man on campus in HS, if you were going to tell me that my college roommate would be gay, I would have said you're crazy. Just another example of not judging a book by its cover. It's wonderful that the time we were roommates has left a lasting impact on me.
>
> Thanks again.
>
> Be well

Understand, accept, and respect.

That's all that needs to be said.

14.

It's About Personal Freedom;

It's About Being Better People

The essence of this country is live and let live. For you to be free means that others need to be free. For example, you are free to follow your religious beliefs that homosexuality is an abomination. But you have to let others be free to follow their own religious beliefs that God loves equally all his creatures, including practicing homosexuals.

You are free to show the world your affection for your spouse. Others should be free to do the same. You are free to choose who you want to marry without the government telling you NO. Others should have the same freedom.

But you are not free to cause bodily or psychological harm to others.

You should not stop others from having the same rights as you do, or vote against them having the same rights that you have.

So this book is about freedom. And it is also about being better people.

It's about respecting others' choices—giving them freedom, even if you disagree. You may not want physical love with somebody of the same gender. But we should respect and celebrate the fact that two people love each other—even if they are the same gender.

Being better people is about knowing that we are *not judging*. It is not about tolerating others, but about celebrating their freedom to be unique—maybe very different from you or from the majority, but still unique, with their virtues and faults, like each of us.

Being a better person, being free and respecting the personal freedom of others, and being treated equally under the law is the fundamental essence that all of us who love our country share in common.

15.

Summary: Who Are These LGBT People?

In the preceding chapters. we have learned a little bit more about lesbian, gay, bisexual, and transgender individuals. In summary, LGBT people are not alien to our lives. They are our neighbors, paramedics, firefighters, elected officials, military personnel, writers, police officers, and others in all professions, backgrounds, and locations. They are also people who have made very important contributions to society in the military, the sciences, the arts, and many other fields. We have seen that you cannot call homosexuality or bisexuality unnatural, since it happens everyday in nature. Science also agrees that homosexuality is not a disease, and that there is nothing to cure, nor is there any effective method to change an individual's sexual orientation.

We have also seen that although the Bible can be interpreted as saying that homosexual acts are an abomination, not everybody agrees with that interpretation. (But if you do, then to be consistent you cannot commit any other abomination such as eating shrimp.)

Freedom of religion is very important. And exactly because different religions have different interpretations about homosexuality, we cannot impose one religion over another when we create *civil laws*. We all agree that each religion is free to marry or to consecrate as ministers or bishops whomever they want.

Further, we've learned that the issue is not whether homosexuality is a choice: religion is included in all of our nondiscrimination legislation (as it should be), and religion is clearly a personal choice.

Finally, we've seen that family values are defined by each family. And for many families, a most important value is that they want all their children to be treated equally—independently of their sexual orientation or gender identity or expression.

Now that we know who these LGBT people are, it is time to examine the Gay Agenda. What do lesbian, gay, bisexual, and transgender individuals want? Do they want special rights? These and other questions will be explored in the next chapters.

Part II:

Which Gay Agenda?

16.

Special Rights

Does anyone deserve special rights?

Think about it.

Commit to an answer.

My answer is this:

Yes, some people deserve special rights.

What?

You got it right: some people do deserve special rights. Take for example, a married couple. They get special rights. And they should. Here are some of the special rights married couples get:

- Unlimited tax-free transfer of assets between spouses (including at death)

- Filing taxes jointly

- Making medical decisions for each other and their children

- Social security benefits after death of a spouse

- Funeral and bereavement leave

- Ability to file wrongful death claims

- Spousal communications privilege that protects confidential communications between spouses during civil and criminal cases

- Spousal testimonial privilege that allows spouses not to testify against each other in a court of law

- Ability to sponsor the other spouse for immigration to the United States

- Joint adoption and foster care

- Automatic legal status with stepchildren

These are just some of the 1,138 special rights that married people get (as detailed in a report by the United States General Accounting Office dated January 23, 2004). And they should get them.

There are also special rights conferred to some people as protections against discrimination or hate crimes. These special rights are based on characteristics at birth that cannot be changed such as race, gender, and country of origin. But the special protections are also based on characteristics that are, and should be, a personal choice, such as choice of religion.

So, LGBT people are not seeking special rights that nobody else receives—just to be treated like people in similar circumstances.

But if you are not gay, why should you care about gay rights? You might be surprised by some of the reasons, discussed in the following chapter.

17.

If I Am Not Gay, Why Should I Care About Gay Rights?

Because the crucial issue is not about gay rights; it is about who we are as a country and as good human beings. Do we give personal freedom to others to be themselves and be treated like everybody else without fear for their life, or their job, just for who they are or what they believe? It is all about basic human rights.

Also, you should care if you have young children or grandchildren. They already have a sexual orientation (heterosexual, homosexual, or bisexual), even if they are too young to know. We have already discussed that tough love and conversion therapies do not work. Wouldn't you then want a world in which they are treated equally under the law, independently of their sexual orientation and gender identity and expression?

Another example why you should care about equal rights for everybody: Say that you are heterosexual and a great accountant who wants to work for an LGBT organization that provides great benefits, and it is close to your home. You should not be discriminated because of your sexual orientation—you should be able to work for a gay organization. Discrimination on the basis of sexual orientation (heterosexual, homosexual, or bisexual) should not be allowed, and the same goes for gender identity (the gender you identify with) and expression (how do you express your gender).

One more example: Imagine you are outside a public restroom holding your wife's purse. You are 100 percent heterosexual, but some thugs think that because you are holding a purse, you are homosexual, and they attack you as they shout "Faggot! Faggot! Here is what you deserve!" This is a true story.

Nobody deserves to be a victim of a hate crime. Thanks to legislation passed by Congress and signed into law in 2009 by President Obama, you are protected against hate crimes because of your religion, race, national origin, gender, sexual orientation, gender identity and expression, and disability.

Now that you care about equal rights for everybody, what's the gay agenda? We'll get closer to an answer in the next chapter, which outlines a gay congressman's agenda.

18.

Barney Frank's Radical Homosexual Agenda

Barney Frank is the most senior openly gay member of Congress. He has been a congressman for more than thirty years and was chairman of the powerful House Financial Services Committee for four years. He has announced that he will retire in January 2013 at age seventy-two. He is considered by many to be a very savvy legislator. He is a graduate of Harvard University and Harvard Law School.

On December 22, 2010—four days after Congress repealed Don't Ask, Don't Tell—Congressman Frank addressed during a press conference what others called the Barney Frank Radical Homosexual Agenda. He said that this agenda was,

1. To be protected against violent crimes driven by bigotry.

2. To be able to get married.

3. To be able to get a job.

4. To be able to fight for our country.

And he added, "For those who are worried about the Radical Homosexual Agenda, let me put them on notice—two down, two to go." As for the "two down," he was referring to the repeal of Don't Ask, Don't Tell, and the expansion of federal hate-crimes legislation to include sexual orientation and gender identity and expression. The "two to go" referred to the right to get married and to employment nondiscrimination.

As much as he is respected, and as much as his speech was wonderful and punchy, this is not the gay agenda. As the next chapter discusses, we need to think bigger.

19.

Thinking *Bigger*

Congressman Frank's "Two down, two to go" should be more like, "One and a half down, several more to go."

The "one" that is "down" is the hate crimes protection that was achieved (at the federal level) when President Obama signed into law the Matthew Shepard and James Byrd Jr. Hate Crimes Prevention Act on October 28, 2009. A caveat: this legislation, while very useful, is not a replacement for state hate-crimes legislation, which is really needed in each state.

A goal that is half down is for service members serving openly in the military. As we explain in chapter 24, these service members can still be discriminated against, and transgender service members are still not allowed to serve their country.

In terms of the two to go, Congressman Frank is referring to marriage and employment nondiscrimination. But there are more than two goals that need to be achieved, including bullying and safety in the schools, parenting rights, and nondiscrimination in housing, financing, public accommodations, and federal government programs.

The LGBT movement, while making significant progress (especially in the states, courts, and public opinion), suffers from not thinking big enough. We saw that Barney Frank's "Radical Homosexual Agenda" was incomplete. For some people, the approach is: *ask for little—get even less.*

So, what's the real Gay Agenda? The true Gay Agenda is disclosed in detail in the next chapter...

20.

Q: What's the Gay Agenda?

A: The American Agenda: Equal Treatment under the Law

The Gay Agenda is very simple: being treated equally under the law, which happens to be the American Agenda and what made America such a great country.

Just look at the laws (federal and state)—whenever you see protections based on race, gender, national origin, and religion, just add the words *sexual orientation* and *gender identity*.

That's it. As Harvey Milk said,

> All men are created equal. No matter how hard you try, you can never erase those words.

If you have read the previous chapters of this book you know that

- Nobody is asking for special rights. LGBT people just want to be treated like other groups. No need to create special legislation for us. Just add "sexual orientation and gender identity" to existing legislation.

- Nobody is comparing the suffering of different groups protected under the law. People have suffered tremendous discrimination and prejudice because of their race. People have suffered tremendous discrimination and prejudice because of their gender, and because of their national origin, and because of their religion, and because of their sexual orientation, and because of their gender identity.

- Nobody wants to curtail your freedom of religion. Some religions support LGBT equality, while others oppose it. The government cannot pick one religion over another. So public policy is based on treating everybody equally under the law. Each religion has the right to decide whom to marry, whom to allow to remarry in that faith, or who to elevate to priesthood, among other rights.

- Whether being LGBT is a choice or not is irrelevant in this discussion. Religion clearly is a personal choice and it is (and should be) protected against discrimination. Similarly, sexual orientation and gender identity and expression should be protected, too.

So what are the areas of the law in which LGBT people are not treated equally?

- Hates crimes
- Nondiscrimination
- Military
- Marriage equality
- Freedom of gender
- Protecting youth
- Same-gender parenting

Each of these areas is an Equality Goal—what needs to be done to be treated equally under the law. Each Equality Goal is discussed in detail in the successive chapters.

One point to note before we proceed: Some people can debate that the real Gay Agenda is social justice or to be equal in real life, not just under the law. This is a very honorable objective. But, as we have seen in prior chapters, real equality comes very slowly, even after legal equality is reached. For example, forty-five years after interracial marriage was made legal in all fifty states by the Supreme Court, some people still oppose it (a significant number of people, in some states).

For the real, long-term gay agenda do not miss reading the Epilogue. The immediate focus of our energy is on legal equality under the law. How difficult is this to achieve?

21.

It's Not Rocket Science

Some problems are very difficult. Launching a rocket to the moon, landing it there, and bringing the astronauts safely home is a very difficult problem. And we are the only country in the world to have solved it. Overhauling the medical system in a country is a difficult problem. Treating everybody equally under the law is not a difficult problem to solve. Here is how it can be done:

1. Examine the areas of the law in which lesbian, gay, bisexual, and transgender individuals are not treated equally. Call these areas Equality Goals. (This is simple, yet organizations still talk about issues instead of goals—just check their websites.)

2. Create a way to measure progress at the federal level and in each of the states—so you can eventually claim more accurately how many have been achieved instead of saying "two down, two to go," as Representative Frank claimed.

3. Write these Equality Goals in legal terms. You can put it all into an omnibus bill. Whether you seek passage as one bill or as a collection of bills is not as critical. An omnibus bill shows, in legal terms, what we need to achieve. It also shows that we are not seeking special rights, because the main thing that we are doing is adding the terms *sexual orientation* and *gender identity* in places in current law that protect race, gender, national origin, and religion.

4. Identify the different paths that there are to achieve each goal: via the legislatures, via the courts, and via popular vote. Different people and different organizations will take different paths to achieve each of the Equality Goals. Insofar as we are all in agreement on the goals, this is fine because it is very difficult to know in advance which path will lead us to equality faster.

5. Endorse candidates for elected office with clear criteria. A good endorsement process needs to result in more than just an endorse-or-don't-endorse outcome. It is also important to make the endorsement criteria public.

6. Monitor politicians to ensure that, once elected, these endorsed candidates indeed are taking action and sponsoring and voting for equality legislation.

7. Ensure that you bring on board *all* the people affected.

So, understanding what needs to be done is not rocket science. The following chapters examine each of the steps, starting with each of the Equality Goals to be achieved.

22.

Equality Goal: Hate-Crimes Legislation

There are many misunderstandings about hate-crimes legislation:

CLAIM: If a crime is already penalized, there's no need to penalize more because the motivation was hate.

REALITY: Penalties imposed by the judicial system are usually based on motivation and intent. If someone kills somebody by accident, the penalty is less severe than if there was premeditation. Likewise, the penalty should be different when the motivation was hate.

CLAIM: Sexual orientation concerns a special group, and therefore, sexual orientation does not need to be protected under the law.

REALITY: The law already protects other special groups subject to attack (for example, due to religious beliefs). The law needs to protect sexual-orientation and gender-identity victims, because about the same number of them are attacked per year as are those attacked due to their religious beliefs. In addition, sexual orientation covers, by definition, heterosexuals in addition to homosexuals and bisexuals.

CLAIM: Sexual orientation is a choice (is not innate), so it should not be protected.

REALITY: Science demonstrates that sexual orientation is innate. But even if it was a choice, it should be protected since religious beliefs (which are clearly a choice) are already protected.

CLAIM: Pastors may be tried under this legislation if, after their giving a sermon, a member of the congregation, motivated by the sermon, commits a hate crime.

REALITY: The hate-crimes legislation explicitly includes First Amendment protections toward speech. Hate crimes legislation is about actions and bodily harm against somebody. Speech is still protected, we are always free to think and talk, even hateful speech. This legislation was supported, among others, by the Presbyterian and Episcopal churches.

CLAIM: Federal hate crimes legislation means that the federal government will be interfering with local police.

REALITY: The hate-crimes legislation has been endorsed by virtually all major law enforcement organizations (including the International Association of Chiefs of Police, the National District Attorneys Association, the National Sheriffs Association, the Police Executive Research Forum, etc.). The police force understands the hideousness of these crimes and wants to have sexual orientation and gender identity and expression in the federal hate-crime laws.

Why is investigating and penalizing hate crimes is so important?

The FBI has a very clear statement about hate crimes on its website:

> Investigating hate crime is the number one priority of our Civil Rights Program. Why? Not only because hate crime has a devastating impact on families and communities, but also because groups that preach hatred and intolerance plant the seeds of terrorism here in our country.

The most recent FBI statistics indicate that in 2009 there were 1,482 victims of hate crimes in the United States due to sexual orientation. This is about the same number of victims (1,575) due to religion. It is very important to cover in legislation both types of hate crimes.

Since 1968, there has been a federal hate crimes law that penalizes violent crimes against individuals due to their race, religion, and ethnic origin. It is well understood that there should be an additional penalty when somebody hurts somebody intentionally motivated by hate toward the race or ethnic origin or religion of the victim.

However, for forty-one years there was no federal hate-crimes legislation covering such obvious targets as gender and disability.

In 2005, legislation extending those protections to include gender, disability, sexual orientation, and gender identity and expression was introduced and was approved by the House, but was not voted by the Senate. It was reintroduced in 2007, but it stalled after President G.W. Bush threatened to veto it. Finally, in 2009 it was approved by Congress. President Obama signed the Matthew Shepard and James Byrd Jr. Hate Crimes Prevention Act on October 28, 2009.

This federal law was named after two well-publicized hate-crimes victims who suffered horrifying deaths: James Byrd Jr. was a heterosexual African American who was dragged from a pick up truck by three white supremacists in Texas. He was conscious through most of the ordeal, until his head and arm were severed when hitting a curb. The three supremacists continued to drive the truck, dragging the headless body for more than a mile. At that time, in 1998, Texas did not have a hate-crime statute (now it has one but it does not cover gender identity or expression). The second person for whom the bill is named is Matthew Shepard, a gay student who, also in 1998, was beaten and left to die on a fence in Laramie, Wyoming. At the time, Wyoming did not have any hate-crime statutes either, and still does not have one.

Although equality and protection of people would be expected to be a nonpartisan issue, the Matthew Shepard and James Byrd Jr. Hate Crimes Prevention Act passed Congress in a very partisan manner.

- In the House of Representatives, the vote was 249 in favor to 175 opposed. Of the votes in favor, 93 percent were cast by Democrats. Of the votes against the legislation, 90 percent were from Republicans.

- In the Senate the vote was 63 to 28 (with 9 senators not voting). Of the 63 senators voting in favor, 92 percent were Democrats or Independents (senators Lieberman and Sanders); while all of the 28 Senators voting against it were Republicans.

The statistics above may appear partisan. The reality is that equality is still a partisan matter in the United States: the majority of Democratic legislators vote in favor of equality, while the majority of Republican legislators vote against it. We will see the same reality as we discuss all the Equality Goals.

But equality should not be a partisan matter. Legislators of any party affiliation should agree to what the population already agrees: *everybody* should be treated *equally* under the law. A Hart Research poll in 2007 (two years before the legislation was passed) showed that 73 percent of Americans supported hate-crime legislation covering sexual orientation and gender identity and expression. More interestingly:

- 56 percent of Republican men supported hate crimes legislation, and

- 63 percent of Evangelical Christians supported it too

Americans understand that sexual orientation protection covers everybody, since every person is either heterosexual, homosexual, or bisexual. Fortunately, now we have a federal hate-crimes statute. This helps in the states, but it is *not* a replacement for legislation in each state:

- Only fourteen states and the District of Columbia have hate-crime statutes covering sexual orientation and gender identity and expression.

- Sixteen additional states cover only sexual orientation.

- Twenty states do not have hate-crime statutes covering sexual orientation or gender identity and expression. Note that thirty-six states do not cover gender identity or expression.

This Equality Goal has been achieved at the federal level, but still lots of work remains to be done in the states. Let's examine another very important Equality Goal in the next chapter.

23.

Equality Goal: Nondiscrimination

Mary gets to work to find a note from her boss to see him immediately. Upon entering his office, she can tell that something is wrong.

The boss tells her that she is being fired. She says, "You mean, laid off." The boss says—"No, you are being fired. No layoff package. No unemployment benefits."

Mary is in shock. She thinks about the twelve years she has spent with the company in Florida. In her mind she goes through the annual raises, the promotions, the wonderful reviews.

She tells the boss, "Tell it to me straight. Why I am getting fired?" The boss doesn't want to tell. But finally, having known Mary for so many years, he talks. The boss says, "My new boss told me that he doesn't want dykes working here."

Mary calls a friend who is an attorney. The attorney says: "I do not need to think about the case very much." Mary is intrigued. The attorney friend continues. "There is absolutely nothing that anyone can do."

Mary is confused. In her state of Florida, like in the majority of states, if the company would have dismissed her by saying that her performance was not good enough, she could have fought it in court by asking them to prove it—given that her annual performance reviews clearly said the contrary. But because she was dismissed simply for being a lesbian, there is nothing that she can do. Sexual orientation and gender identity and expression are not protected in her state. Nor is it protected at the federal level.

Protection for sexual orientation also means protection if you are discriminated for being heterosexual. Say that you are a bartender working in California in a gay bar and you get fired because you are heterosexual (this actually happened). Because California has a nondiscrimination statute that covers sexual orientation and gender identity and expression, the heterosexual bartender got his job back because you do not need to be gay to be a good bartender in a gay bar.

One of the groups that suffers the most discrimination is people whose gender does not match their gender at birth. Transgender people get severely discriminated in employment, housing, access to public assistance, and so many aspects vital to everyday life. So it is absolutely critical that when seeking equality under the law, we always include sexual orientation *and* gender identity and expression.

Fortunately, on April 20, 2012, the Equal Employment Opportunity Commission in a unanimous ruling decided that transgender individuals were covered under Title VII of the Civil Rights Act related to employment nondiscrimination. This ruling is notable too because the decision was unanimous, and commissioners were appointed by both Republican and Democratic presidents. So, after this important decision, the message to our transgender friends is: please do not leave your gay, lesbian, and bisexual friends behind!

The protections in the United States against discrimination are extensive, as one would expect in an advanced democracy. They include:

- Employment
- Housing
- Credit
- Public accommodation
- Public facilities
- Federally funded programs and activities

A comprehensive bill to protect against discrimination due to sexual orientation was introduced in 1974 in the House of Representatives by Congresswoman Bella Abzug. Year after year it was getting more co-sponsors but it never got voted on. Fifteen years later it was re-introduced focusing only on employment nondiscrimination covering sexual orientation under the strategy that a smaller legislation would have a higher chance to pass. Despite this strategy of asking for less, almost forty years later, there is still no federal law against discrimination in employment due to sexual orientation.

Interestingly, most Americans believe that sexual orientation and gender identity and expression are already protected against discrimination in federal legislation and state laws. Here is the reality:

- There is no federal law protecting against discrimination based on sexual orientation or gender identity and expression.

- In twenty-nine states there is no protection against discrimination based on sexual orientation or gender identity or expression.

- In only fifteen states and the District of Columbia there is protection against discrimination based on sexual orientation and gender identity and expression.

- Six states provide limited protection.

As of April 20, 2012, transgender individuals are the only LGBT people protected nationwide against employment discrimination thanks to an Equal Employment Opportunity Commission ruling.

However, there is much work to be done to achieve the protection against discrimination in employment, housing, credit, public accommodation, public facilities and federal funded programs that most Americans take for granted (and falsely believe is already available to lesbian, gay, bisexual, and transgender people). Three main things need to be done:

First, and the easiest, the president needs to sign an executive order protecting federal employees and contractors of the federal government against discrimination based on sexual orientation and gender identity and expression. Currently, there is Executive Order 13087 signed by President Clinton in 1998 that protects only federal employees (not federal contractors) and only for sexual orientation (does not include gender identity or expression). There is also Executive Order 11246 signed by President Johnson in 1965, which prohibits federal contractors from discriminating on the basis of race, color, religion, sex, or national origin.

As a presidential candidate in 2008, Barack Obama promised that he would sign such an executive order covering federal employees and contractors (a total of twenty-six million people or about 20 percent of the working population), as reported by *Metro Weekly* (March 8, 2012). Apparently, such an executive order has been drafted and vetted, and it is ready for President Obama's signature. An April 2011 poll by the Center for American Progress showed that 69 percent of 2012 likely voters support President Obama issuing such an executive order (this includes 83 percent of Democrats, 69 percent of Independents, and 53 percent of Republicans). So, no more delays!

This executive order is important, because then the performance of the contractors in terms of nondiscrimination for sexual orientation and gender identity and expression is part of the regular reviews performed by the Labor Department's Office of Federal Contract Compliance Programs. This is an independent review of complaints brought up by employees, many of whom are reluctant to file formal complaints.

Second, we need to pass federal nondiscrimination legislation that covers sexual orientation and gender identity and expression. Given how committees in Congress work, it might be necessary to have separate legislation covering, respectively, employment, housing, credit, public accommodation, public facilities, and federally funded programs and activities.

The main question is, do we proceed for each of these bills as a separate bill or as a modification of the Civil Rights Act? The current approach, favored by most organizations, is to have a separate bill. Some people believe that the Civil Rights Act should not be expanded to cover other groups, or that opening it for debate may bring undesirable changes. The reality is that Title VII has been expanded in the past to prohibit discrimination due to pregnancy (1978). President Obama could simply state that he would support an expansion of the Civil Rights Act to include sexual orientation and gender identity and expression, but would veto any other modifications that would limit existing rights to any other group. The president, so far, is not providing such important leadership, although he is much better than Romney, who opposes federal nondiscrimination legislation. Nondiscrimination legislation is supported by a majority of Republican voters and an even larger majority of Democratic voters.

If pursuing the route of a separate bill, we need to watch that the exemptions given to religious organizations and corporations are the same as the ones given in the Civil Rights Act. Exemptions are usually added to bills at the last moment, often for the worse. There is a possibility that with a separate bill, we could get some clauses that are more advantageous to the LGBT community than what would be available with the Civil Rights Act, but this is not the Gay Agenda: we want legal equality—the same rights as other groups. So the most coherent solution is to add "sexual orientation and gender identity" to existing nondiscrimination federal legislation.

In October 2007, Representative Barney Frank, who is the senior LGBT member in Congress, decided to strip gender identity and expression protections from the Employment Nondiscrimination Act that he was proposing for a vote. This was an awakening call for the movement for LGBT equality. In a matter of days, more than three hundred organizations signed up opposing such a move. The National Gay and Lesbian Task Force (TheTaskForce.org) and the National Center for Transgender Equality (TransEquality.org) took the lead. In the meantime, it took the Human Rights Campaign (HRC.org), the largest LGBT organization, eighteen months to come on board.

In the fall of 2011, a new organization, Freedom To Work (FreedomToWork.org), was founded. It focuses on passing employment nondiscrimination legislation, and it has already brought significant experience to this fight. From the corporate side, OutAndEqual.org is dedicated to creating safe and equitable workplaces for LGBT employees.

Third, we need to pass nondiscrimination legislation or make it comprehensive in the thirty-five states that lack it. Even if we pass the federal Employment Nondiscrimination Act or, better, add sexual orientation and gender identity to the Civil Rights Act, the reality is that state legislation is still needed. The main reason is that in many cases it is much easier to file suit at the state level. Another reality is that in some states the state statutes are stronger than the federal ones. However, states that currently do not have nondiscrimination statutes for sexual orientation and gender identity are not expected to create stronger ones than those the federal administration proposes.

Nondiscrimination is a critical battle for equality in our country because it affects so many people. Also, people cannot fight for other rights if they are concerned that they will be fired for being who they are. It is a tough battle to gain traction since so many Americans think that sexual orientation and gender identity must already be part of any nondiscrimination statute, while it is not at the federal level and in most states. So the battle continues on this front, but we got a sliver of equality in one of the most important institutions in our country—read on!

24.

Equality Goal: Serving in the Military

Finally, on September 20, 2011, the repeal of Don't Ask, Don't Tell took effect. This was the legislation passed in 1993 that forced many service members, who are risking their lives for our freedom, to have to live a lie. The support for repeal had become just too big to ignore: 77 percent of Americans supported the repeal (*Washington Post/ABC News* poll, 12/15/2010).

The legislation to repeal Don't Ask, Don't Tell was passed in December 2010:

- The House of Representatives voted 250 to 175 for the repeal. Of those voting in favor, 94 percent were Democrats and 6 percent were Republicans. Of those voting against the repeal, 91 percent were Republicans and 9 percent Democrats.

- The Senate voted 65 to 33 for repeal. Of those voting in favor, 88 percent were Democrats or Independents, and 12 percent were Republicans. Of those voting against the repeal, 100 percent were Republican.

However, to gain some Republican support the legislation was modified at the last moment to eliminate the clause that stated that service members cannot be discriminated because of their sexual orientation. It is very different to be allowed to disclose your sexual orientation (which is the new policy) than to ensure that are you are protected against discrimination.

While repealing Don't Ask Don't Tell was momentous, we were let down by a Congress that did only half the job. It took more than seventeen years to get to this point. How many more years until we add sexual orientation to the nondiscrimination policies of the military?

Here is what is left to accomplish:

1. Enact legislation that specifically protects against discrimination based on sexual orientation/gender identity in the military.

2. Revise the Department of Defense Equal Opportunity Policy to add sexual orientation and gender identity.

3. Amend military medical and uniform regulations that discriminate against transgender service members. This is included as part of the Freedom of Gender Equality Goal.

4. Depenalize sodomy, as ruled by the US Supreme Court in *Lawrence v Texas* by revoking article 125 of the Uniform Code of Military Justice (UCMJ). Article 125 forbids sodomy whether among people of the same gender or different gender. Congress needs to revoke article 125, as the military has been requesting for years, since it is clearly understood that what consenting adults do in private is exactly that, private.

5. Treat all married service members equally. There are still significant differences in treatment based on same-gender or different-gender marriages. While this is mostly due to the Defense of Marriage Act, the reality is that the Department of Defense has leeway that other departments do not.

6. To fully achieve equality in the military will require Congress to act again, otherwise a future administration could ban LGBT members from serving by using a directive from the Department of Defense—without need for an act of Congress or an Executive Order from the president.

For an up-to-date analysis of what still needs to be done, you can check the list maintained by Captain (ret) Tom Carpenter, Esq. at www.eQualityGiving.org/DADT

If Congress doesn't act, another venue is the lawsuit that the Log Cabin Republicans are pursuing with the intention of proving to the Supreme Court, if necessary, that discrimination of LGBT people in the military is unconstitutional.

Many organizations got involved in the repeal of Don't Ask, Don't Tell, but two of them played a key, long-term role in the repeal: the Service members Legal Defense Network (SLDN.org) and the Palm Center (PalmCenter.org). Both of them are likely to redefine their mission in the near future. In the meantime, a new organization, OutServe.org, created in October 2009, will merge in October 2012 with SLDN.

In addition, several individuals led by Lt. Dan Choi and assisted by a new organization, GetEqual.org, added tremendous visibility to the fight not only with the public, but also with elected officials, including President Obama and Senate Majority Leader Reid.

Time to discuss another Equality Goal—let's get married!

25.

Equality Goal: Marriage Equality

The freedom to marry is the most prominent battle for equality in our country today. It has caught the imagination of a young generation, who cannot comprehend such discrimination. So most people might expect this to be the longest chapter of the book.

It isn't.

Because the argument couldn't be simpler: It represents the essence of who we are as a country. Marriage equality represents freedom of religion and the pursuit of happiness. It represents the ideal that we live and let live. It represents that we encourage people's taking care of each other in a lifelong commitment. It represents the idea that we do not want the government to dictate who we can marry.

There are five main arguments that are used to deny people the fundamental right to marry the person they love:

1. *"My religion says that marriage is between one man and one woman forever."*
   This is a very valid argument. You have all the right to believe so. Nobody can impose on your religion to marry same-gender couples or to allow divorces.

   At the same time, other religions believe that marriage is between two people who love each other—even if they are the same gender.

   So how do we allow you your freedom of religion and at the same time allow others their freedom of religion?

   It is quite simple: each religion can impose any constraints they want on whom to marry. We do not want the government to impose of you the wishes of another religion. So, the government issues *civil* marriage *licenses* according to its own criteria—one that treats all the citizens the same independently of their religion or their sexual orientation and gender identity and expression.

2. *"What about the sanctity of marriage?"*
Many religions consider marriage to be sacred. Naturally, only those couples who have married in that church according to the church teachings are bound by that sacred relationship. But people married in a civil marriage chose to be bound by civil laws and not by religious law in their marriage. Civil marriage and religious marriage are totally different.

3. *"For three thousand years, marriage has been between one man and one woman."*
This is the argument presented by Mitt Romney. It shows a complete ignorance of our history: several Native American tribes were polygamous. The Mormon Church supported "plural marriages" (one man, several women) until 1890. After such marriages were forbidden, Mitt Romney's grandfather moved the family to a polygamous commune in Mexico. So, marriage has *not* been between one man and one woman for three thousand years. And Mitt Romney knows that very well.

4. *"Why not confer the same obligations and benefits of marriage except for the word marriage? Why not just have civil unions?"*
This was the position of President Obama until he evolved on May 9, 2012. Civil unions are a different institution, which is separate and discriminatory. It is a separate statute from marriage, and we have learned in our country that separate is not equal. It is also discriminatory because it only applies to LGBT people.

5. *"Isn't marriage an issue for the states?"*
Marriage is indeed based on state law, but it is also a federal issue.

First, we need to repeal the Defense of Marriage Act (DOMA), which forbids the federal government from recognizing otherwise legal marriages of same-gender couples. Obviously, it is outrageous that the federal government won't recognize all the marriage licenses issued by a state.

Second, we need to ensure that a couple legally married is recognized anywhere in the country. Imagine that you are a heterosexual couple, and that your marriage was not recognized in certain states. What would happen to your freedom to travel and relocate?

A well-respected Republican pollster, Jan van Lohuizen, found out that until 2009, support for gay marriage was increasing at a rate of 1 percent per year. Since then it is increasing at 5 percent per year across all age groups and party affiliations.

Many organizations are involved in achieving this goal especially all the LGBT legal organizations, in addition to Freedom To Marry (FreedomToMarry.org) which specializes on this Equality Goal.

We can have freedom of religion while letting all loving and committed couples take care of each other. Let's move on to other Equality Goals.

26.

Equality Goal: Freedom of Gender

The majority of people understand the reality that sexual orientation is clearly part of a spectrum ranging from heterosexuality to homosexuality with a middle ground of bisexuality.

However, most people see gender identity as clearly binary: you are either male or female. The reality is that this is not what happens in nature. While the vast majority of us are either male or female, the Intersex Society of North America estimates that: "the total of people whose bodies differ from standard male or female is one in 100 births." This is a complex medical issue that goes well beyond having a Y chromosome or not.

You may have not heard of intersex before and therefore wonder whether this is a new condition. Since this appears naturally, it is not a new condition. Actually, a great sculpture can be found at the Louvre Museum. It shows a beautiful female naked body over a marble mattress, with a female figure but with male genitalia. The sculpture is called the Sleeping Hermaphrodite ("Hermaphrodite Endormi"). It is about 1,800 years old.

Not everybody is clearly male or female from a physical perspective. Similarly, there are people who know that their true gender is not the gender of their birth. As an advanced society, with knowledge based on scientific analysis, we understand the need that some people have to live their true gender.

Transgender and intersex are different conditions, and organizations fighting for the rights of transgender people and intersex people try to keep them as separate issues. We respect this, but note that in both cases they suffer tremendous discrimination and prejudices from so many people who are not familiar with the facts.

Similarly, some people are uncomfortable when people do not behave in the expected roles of male or female. This is called gender expression. Maybe a female who is "too butch" or a male who is "too effeminate" or a person who is not intersex nor transgender but who likes to dress in a non-gender-conforming manner.

Many people feel more comfortable with a binary world ("black or white"), but this is not the real world or the world of nature.

Here are some of the hurdles and discriminatory treatment that people face about their gender identity or expression:

- Employment discrimination
- Lack of healthcare access and insurance coverage
- Inability to declare the appropriate gender in documents (passport, driver's license, social security database, and voting ID) to avoid confusion in real life.
- Access to restrooms
- Air travel scrutiny
- Gender stereotyping
- Military medical and uniform regulations that discriminate transgender service members

You may have some misgivings about giving people the freedom of gender. Some of these misgivings may be rooted in your religious beliefs. You certainly have the right to have those beliefs. Other people have the religious belief that God created a complex natural environment with many variations of gender identity and expression and sexual orientation.

There are some notable organizations working on this goal of freedom of gender: the National Center for Transgender Equality (TransEquality.org), the TransgenderLawCenter.org, and, from the broader perspective of sexual freedom as a fundamental human right, the Woodhull Sexual Freedom Alliance (WoodhullAlliance.org).

We all share a common respect for our Constitution and the belief of not letting the government interfere in our most intimate decisions. Because of that we need to ensure that people with a different gender identity or expression are treated equally under the law and can pursue their personal happiness free from discrimination.

Now let's look into the next Equality Goal in the following chapter.

27.

Equality Goal: Protecting Youth

One of our obligations in society, in places of worship, in families, and in schools is to protect our youth.

We have to do much better.

What are the effects on LGBT youth when they become homeless because their parents throw them out of the house, while still underage, for being gay? What happens when schools are not allowed to teach about sexual orientation, or cannot teach about protections to avoid pregnancy and sexually transmitted diseases? What happens when children, and especially LGBT children, are mistreated in the foster care system? What happens when LGBT youth hear the repeated anti-equality messages from so many elected officials? from their teachers? from their parents? What happens when heterosexual children are mistreated just because their parents are LGBT?

Are we a society who cares about our youth or not? Do we provide the safe space in which they can develop to their full potential? Studies show that 85 percent of LGBT students in middle and high school suffered from harassment in the prior school year (check GLSEN.org for their pioneering research). Harassment does not lend itself to a safe environment for youth to study, grow, and develop.

Too many young people have suffered due to some wrong-headed beliefs and actions from some elected public officials, some parents, some educators, some church leaders, and other people who are supposed to help our youth. In 2010 all of this came to a head. In July that year, Justin Aaberg, age 15, died by suicide in Minnesota. In September, it was Tyler Clementi, 18, a freshman at Rutger's, and Billy Lucas, 15, from Indiana, also died by suicide. There was a national outrage, which resulted in a White House summit on bullying. An important resource to recommend to youth in distress is TheTrevorProject.org.

More than twenty-five years ago, Harvey Milk, the openly gay member of the San Francisco Board of Supervisors who was killed in 1978 by another member of that Board, put it best:

> And the young gay people in the Altoona, Pennsylvanias and the Richmond, Minnesotas who are coming out and hear Anita Bryant in television and her story. The only thing they have to look forward to is hope. And you have to give them hope. Hope for a better world, hope for a better tomorrow, hope for a better place to come to if the pressures at home are too great. Hope that all will be all right. Without hope, not only gays, but the blacks, the seniors, the handicapped, the us'es, the us'es will give up.

We have not solved the problem yet. LGBT youth continue to suffer tremendously. In September 2010, Dan Savage, a gay columnist, and a few days later Joel Burns, City Councilman in Fort Worth, Texas, sent a message of hope to teenagers by stating that *It Gets Better*. The video by Joel was watched more than 2.7 million times, and the video from Dan and his husband Terry, more than 1.7 million times.

As part of the ItGetsBetter.org project, many videos have been created and posted online. Here is a startling comparison about political leaders who made an It Gets Better video and whether their counterparts did or not:

- The President of the United States found the time to make a video for ItGetsBetter.org
- The Vice President of the United States did one too.
- Republican contenders Mitt Romney and Paul Ryan did not.
- Democratic Speaker Nancy Pelosi also made a video.
- Republican Speaker John Boehner did not.

And the list could go on and on. If we cannot take care of all of our children, what type of society are we?

Our obligation to children is to *make it better*. Here is what needs to be done urgently:

1. Pass federal legislation forbidding bullying and harassment in schools for *all* youth. Studies show that this type of

legislation is not only critical for the physical and mental welfare of all students, but also decreases school absence by bullied students. This legislation should specifically list sexual orientation and gender identity and expression. Research by GLSEN.org shows that statutes that do not enumerate specifically sexual orientation and gender identity provide no more benefit to students than not having any law at all.

2. Approve similar legislation in the states. Unfortunately, only eighteen states provide anti-bullying legislation protecting youth because of sexual orientation and gender identity. Depending on the final makeup of federal legislation, state statutes would be still critical.

And here are other tasks that are critical for the appropriate development of LGBT youth:

1. Advocate for reproductive, sexual, and mental health education that is responsible and age-appropriate. Abstinence-until marriage programs have been proven not to work—even less with lesbian, gay, bisexual, and transgender youth, who are not allowed in most states to marry the person they love. AdvocatesForYouth.org is a good organization pursuing this goal.

2. Ensure that Gay Straight Alliances (GSA) are allowed in all schools. The Gay-Straight Alliance Network is supporting GSAs and young leaders nationwide (GSANetwork.org).

3. Repeal legislation in seven states that prohibits portraying homosexuality in a positive light or discussing the contributions to society of so many LGBT people and the issues that LGBT people face. The seven states are: Alabama, Arizona, Mississippi, Oklahoma, South Carolina, Texas, and Utah. For a listing of notable LGBT people and their contributions, check appendix 1.

4. Ensure also the protection of straight children of LGBT parents. COLAGE.org is an organization for youth with a lesbian, gay, bisexual, or transgender parent.

5. Enact legislation protecting LGBT youth in foster care and in the juvenile justice system.

6. Ensure enforcement of all youth protection legislation.

The message to our youth is that *it gets better*. It is true that after the teenage years, things change and do get better, but not because the laws are more equal. Still you can be fired. Still you cannot marry in most states. Still the federal government does not recognize your marriage from one of the few states in which you can get it. And so on.

The responsibility of the adults is to *make it better*. We need to pass anti-bullying legislation to end the torment of so many of our young people. And we also need to show that we have created a society in which everybody is truly treated the same under the law.

Time now for the next chapter to address our last Equality Goal.

28.

Equality Goal: Same-Gender Parenting

Like most couples, many LGBT couples want to form their own families. This is a fundamental human feeling and a basic right. The family structure brings stability to society. For the protection of children, it is very important to have legislation that treats all families equally under the law.

Independent research clearly indicates that same-gender couples are as effective in parenting as different-gender couples. Here is what the American Academy of Pediatrics has to say about it (www.healthychildren.org/English/family-life/family-dynamics/ types-of-families/pages/Gay-and-Lesbian-Parents.aspx):

> Studies have shown that children with gay and/or lesbian parents are ultimately just as happy with themselves and their own gender as are their friends with heterosexual parents. Children whose parents are homosexual show no difference in their choice of friends, activities, or interests compared to children whose parents are heterosexual. As adults, their career choices and lifestyles are similar to those of children raised by heterosexual parents.
>
> Research comparing children raised by homosexual parents to children raised by heterosexual parents has found no developmental differences in intelligence, psychological adjustment, social adjustment, or peer popularity between them. Children raised by homosexual parents can and do have fulfilling relationships with their friends as well as romantic relationships later on.

And here is the conclusion from a report of the American Academy of Pediatrics (neoreviews.aappublications.org/content/pediatrics/ 118/1/349.full):

There is ample evidence to show that children raised by same-gender parents fare as well as those raised by heterosexual parents. More than 25 years of research have documented that there is no relationship between parents' sexual orientation and any measure of a child's emotional, psychosocial, and behavioral adjustment. These data have demonstrated no risk to children as a result of growing up in a family with 1 or more gay parents. Conscientious and nurturing adults, whether they are men or women, heterosexual or homosexual, can be excellent parents. The rights, benefits, and protections of civil marriage can further strengthen these families.

And here is information from the American Psychological Association, in very clear terms (www.apa.org/helpcenter/sexual-orientation.aspx):

Social science has shown that the concerns often raised about children of lesbian and gay parents— concerns that are generally grounded in prejudice against and stereotypes about gay people—are unfounded. Overall, the research indicates that the children of lesbian and gay parents do not differ markedly from the children of heterosexual parents in their development, adjustment, or overall well-being.

Professor Judith Stacey of New York University summarizes it very well (en.wikipedia.org/wiki/LGBT_parenting):

Rarely is there as much consensus in any area of social science as in the case of gay parenting, which is why the American Academy of Pediatrics and all of the major professional organizations with expertise in child welfare have issued reports and resolutions in support of gay and lesbian parental rights.

So the scientific evidence is clear. Despite this, in 2008, the state of Florida spent $120,000 of taxpayers' money for the testimony of Dr. George Alan Rekers, who was paid to testify in opposition to a lawsuit asking to allow single LGBT people to adopt in Florida—

like they can do in *all* other states. Dr. Rekers, a professor and ordained Southern Baptist minister, has written extensively about homosexuality, parenting, and conversion therapy. He also testified on multiple occasions in the past against parenthood by LGBT people, as well as testifying that homosexuality is sinful.

Dr. Rekers was a major player in denying LGBT people their equality. In the ultimate irony and hypocrisy, it was discovered that in May 2010, Dr. Rekers hired a male prostitute from RentBoy.com for a ten-day trip to London and Madrid, with detailed duties for his escort. These duties included sexual massages. Frank Rich wrote in the *New York Times* on May 15, 2010:

> Thanks to Rekers's clownish public exposure, we now know that his professional judgments are windows into *his* cracked psyche, not gay people's. But there is nothing funny about the destruction his writings and public activities have sown. His fringe views have not remained on the fringe. His excursions into public policy have had real and damaging consequences on a large swath of Americans.

The suitability of an individual or a couple to be adoptive parents is always reviewed on a case-by-case basis. However, some states discriminate if the individual or couple is lesbian, gay, bisexual, or transgender, without giving them the opportunity to demonstrate that they can be good parents.

We need equal treatment under the law in the three types of adoption:

1. *Adoption by an individual who is single*
   Florida was the only state in which there was an explicit prohibition for LGBT people to adopt, whether single, or in a relationship. An ACLU lawsuit resulted in a ruling on September 22, 2010, that such a ban was unconstitutional. On October 12, 2010, the Florida Department of Children and Families decided not to appeal the case. Therefore, LGBT people can now adopt legally in the state of Florida.

2. *Adoption by a same-gender couple*
   In ten states and the District of Columbia, there is specific legislation allowing LGBT couples to adopt (California, Connecticut, District of Columbia, Illinois, Indiana, Maine, Massachusetts, New Jersey, New York, Oregon, and Vermont). In addition, in two states (Nevada and New Hampshire) same-sex couples have been able to adopt in some jurisdictions. Mississippi expressly forbids same-gender couples to adopt. Utah does not allow couples not legally married to adopt; since Utah does not recognize same-sex marriages from other states, same-gender couples cannot adopt there.

3. *Adoption by a member of a same-gender couple of the child of the other member (called second-parent adoption)*
   Four states authorize second-parent adoption in their statutes (California, Colorado, Connecticut, and Vermont). In six states and the District of Columbia, appellate courts have determined that second-parent adoption is allowed for same-sex couples (District of Columbia, Illinois, Indiana, Massachusetts, New York, New Jersey, Pennsylvania). In one state, Utah, legislation expressly prohibits second-parent adoption. In three states, appellate courts have determined that second-parent adoption is not allowed for same-sex couples (Nebraska, Ohio, Wisconsin). In the rest of the states, the law is not clear, and in some cases trial courts have allowed second-parent adoption. In Oklahoma, a ban on recognition of same-sex adoptions from other states was challenged and won in court in 2006 by Lambda Legal.

So there is much work to be done in the states to achieve full equality in adoption by same-gender couples. All the major LGBT legal organizations have been involved and have been very successful with adoption cases. These organizations are:

- ACLU Lesbian and Gay Rights Project (ACLU.org/LGBT-rights)

- Gay and Lesbian Defenders & Advocates (GLAD.org)

- Lambda Legal (LambdaLegal.org)

- National Center for Lesbian Rights (NCLRights.org)

But in addition to the work in the states, we need to pass federal legislation. In particular, we need to pass the Every Child Deserves a Family Act, which does not allow discrimination on the basis of sexual orientation, gender identity, or marital status of the prospective adoptive or foster parent or the sexual orientation or gender identity of the child involved. The standard, in every situation, should be based on the best interests of the child.

Given the scientific evidence and the absolute need for more adoptive and foster parents, it is horrible that some people are working so hard to deny these children an opportunity to live in a loving home. Our country is better than that.

29.

Keeping Score

It is critical to keep track of progress towards legal equality. To that effect, eQualityGiving (full disclosure: an organization that I cofounded) pioneered two measurements: one at the federal level and one at the state level.

At the federal level, there are thirteen major areas of federal law in which LGBT people are not treated equally. These areas are basically addressed by the seven Equality Goals, in which some goals are counted separately, since different committees in Congress may consider them. Under this measurement, we have achieved:

- Hate-crime legislation at the federal level. Full goal achieved.

- Repeal of Don't Ask, Don't Tell has been achieved; but there is no protection against discrimination. Partial goal achieved.

- Nondiscrimination in employment has been achieved for transgender people—partial goal achieved.

So the rating is now two out of thirteen (counting partial goals as half a point) or 15 percent—we still have a long way to go to be 100 percent equal under federal law. The reality is that this is not rocket science. We know what needs to be done; it is all written in an Omnibus bill that eQualityGiving engaged attorney Karen Doering to prepare (see next chapter).

Much more progress has been made at the state level—although only in a handful of states. For each state, we keep track of six of the seven Equality Goals (we do not track the goal to serve in the military, since most states actually follow federal law for their National Guard). Two states now have reached a score of 100 percent legal equality for its LGBT citizens. Can you guess which states they are?

If you thought Massachusetts, this was a good logical choice, since it was the first state to offer marriage equality. However, it only scores 83 percent, since they are missing a couple of important protections for transgender people.

The two states that have 100 percent equality for LGBT individuals are Connecticut and Vermont. Three states are very close: California, Iowa, and New Jersey, as is the District of Columbia.

Here is why it is important to keep score with uniform measurements: one large state LGBT organization prepared its own study of progress in its state and concluded that they were in the top five states for protecting LGBT citizens from discrimination. The reality is different: the eQualityGiving measure rates their state at 25 percent out of a maximum of 100 percent.

Do you know where your state stands in LGBT equality?

Take the following quiz:

1. HATE CRIMES: Does your state have hate-crime laws that address violent crimes against individuals due to their sexual orientation *and* gender identity and expression?
   a) Yes
   b) Only sexual orientation is covered in state law
   c) No state law (only federal law)
   d) Don't know

2. NONDISCRIMINATION: Does your state have laws that forbid discrimination in employment for both private and public employers as well as in housing, finance, and public accommodations due to sexual orientation; *and* gender identity and expression?
   a) Yes
   b) Mostly: sexual orientation and gender identity covered with the exception of public accommodation protection for gender identity
   c) Only sexual orientation covered
   d) No state law
   e) Don't know

3. CIVIL MARRIAGE EQUALITY: Does your state have laws allowing same gender couples to marry (i.e., get the same

civil marriage license as different-gender couples?)
a) Yes
b) Civil unions
c) Domestic partnerships
d) No
e) Don't know

4. FREEDOM OF GENDER: Does your state allow a transgender person to obtain a new birth certificate indicating the correct gender?
a) Yes
b) Amended certificate (which shows the prior gender)
c) Decided by court order
d) Depends on city clerk
e) No
f) Don't know

5. PROTECTING YOUTH: Does your state have anti-bullying/anti-harassment laws that specifically list sexual orientation *and* gender identity and expression?
a) Yes
b) Only sexual orientation listed
c) No
d) Don't know

6. SAME-GENDER PARENTING RIGHTS: Does your state allow all qualified LGBT individuals and same-gender couples to jointly adopt as well as second-parent adoption?
a) Yes
b) Only single LGBT people can adopt
c) Only single or joint adoption, but not second-parent adoption
d) Depends on the jurisdiction—some do allow it.
e) Not tested—full extent of parental rights not known.
f) No
g) Don't know

You can check the answers for any state and the District of Columbia here: www.eQualityGiving.org/States-of-Equality-and-Gay-Rights-Scorecard

As the federal and state measurements show, more progress has been made on LGBT legal equality in the states than in the federal government. In two states (Connecticut and Vermont), the answer to all the questions above is *yes*. But, in the other forty-eight states, LGBT people are not treated equally under the law.

Finally, it is also worth keeping track of federal policies that can be changed by the president via executive order, without requiring congressional approval. Their effect is more limited, since another president can easily change the policies or just stop enforcing them. A group of LGBT organizations prepared, documented, and published on the web a list of eighty-two policy changes listed by agency. They delivered it to the Obama transition team in December 2008. They have stopped keeping the web page that tracked progress. Some progress has occurred, but one needs to suspect that the progress falls short of the eighty-two proposals.

Why are we shortchanging our beloved constitution and not providing the equal protection under the law that it promises? The next chapter tackles this question.

30.

Equal Once and For All

In 2005, eQualityGiving created the Equality Goals. As we have seen, this is the simple expression in plain English of what is needed for LGBT people to be equal under the law. Interestingly enough, the majority (if not all) of the LGBT organizations dedicate major sections of their websites to *issues* instead of *goals*. This has an impact on focus, approach, measurements, and what constitutes success. It has an impact on endorsements for elected office as well as the expectations about what these candidates should do once they are elected.

In late 2008, eQualityGiving engaged Karen Doering, a well-respected attorney expert on nondiscrimination legislation, to review federal legislation and prepare a model omnibus legislation to bring equality under the law to LGBT people. The result of her work was the Equality and Religious Freedom Act. It covers thirteen areas of federal law in which we are not yet treated equally:

1. Employment in the private sector
2. Employment in the federal government
3. Housing
4. Public accommodation
5. Public facilities
6. Credit
7. Federally funded programs and activities
8. Education
9. Disability
10. Civil marriage
11. Hate crimes (signed into law on October 28, 2009)
12. Armed forces (the Don't Ask, Don't Tell Repeal Act was signed into law on December 22, 2010)
13. Immigration

Currently, instead of immigration (which is automatic, once the Defense of Marriage Act is repealed), we use adoption as the thirteenth category.

You can download the proposed bill here:
www.eQualityGiving.org/Blueprint-for-LGBT-Equality

Some people say it is not a good idea to introduce an omnibus bill in Congress, since it would have to be divided into pieces and submitted to and get approval from so many different subcommittees. This is true, but here are the important reasons to introduce an omnibus bill:

1. *Putting it in writing.*
   Since we are seeking legal equality, it is obvious that we need to have a proposed bill with all our goals. This constitutes the gold standard of what is missing to be equal under the law.

2. *No more than others.*
   The proposed bill demonstrates that LGBT people do not seek "special rights," as the bill basically adds the terms *sexual orientation* and *gender identity* to existing legislation.

3. *No less than others.*
   This bill also is the standard to compare to partial legislation if approved in smaller pieces. How does a bill compare to the appropriate section of the omnibus bill? Are there any last-minute amendments that compromise our equality? This actually happened in the final negotiations to repeal Don't Ask, Don't Tell—important protections were cut at the last moment, as discussed in chapter 24.

Once you understand the purpose of an omnibus bill, you will understand that cutting parts of it in the name of compromise means that *rights get denied.*

A month after eQualityGiving presented the omnibus bill in April 2009, a freshman member of the House of Representatives, Jared Polis (who is gay), said that he would be interested in sponsoring such a bill. Two years later, in 2011, he was seeking feedback about what to include. As of September 2012, his proposed bill, which is just a compilation of bills that had already been introduced, is pending introduction.

Some legislative efforts are difficult. For instance, creating a healthcare overhaul requires significant knowledge of how the industry operates, its effects on patients, and the various approaches to solving the problem. However, equal rights legislation is not difficult to conceive. What to include? Simply include everything in which LGBT people do not have the same rights as others. This is why it is call omnibus legislation. And make it the gold standard—not just a compilation of bills with their own compromises.

How do we raise awareness of the urgency of equality? Read on.

31.

What Happened in Dallas?

Two dozen activists, donors, strategists, and former executive directors got together in Dallas on the weekend of May 15–17, 2009 and drafted a unique document called "The Dallas Principles."

The essence of the Dallas Principles is simple:

Full LGBT Equality Now. No Delays. No Excuses.

This may appear like an obvious declaration. It was as obvious then as it is now, and it was as relevant then as it is today. However, in the last three years we have heard plenty of excuses to delay equality.

Here is some of the background: Just after President Obama was elected in November 2008, as well as during the transition and early months of his presidency, there was interaction between his team and several LGBT organizations. The expectations were high. Everybody understood that there were important priorities (the economy was in shambles, and his policy priority was healthcare). However, it was clear to some of us that many in the LGBT movement were too willing to wait for "the proper time" to achieve equality, and that they were buying into the administration's approach to do it incrementally over many years, well after addressing the economy and healthcare.

eQualityGiving wanted to motivate everybody to push for equality right then, when the conditions were more favorable than they had been in decades, with pro-equality Democrats controlling the White House, the House, and the Senate.

In this spirit, we contacted several people to join us in Dallas. We were careful to select people who were not currently heads of organizations, and were mindful of having a balanced representation of gender, sexual orientation, gender identity, race, as well as different skills and backgrounds. They all accepted, but some had to cancel at the last moment. They were all eager to push for equality.

Why Dallas? Because it was in the center of the country and allowed the participants, who came from all over the country, to meet midway (nobody except for the moderator was from Dallas). This would ensure that people wouldn't join just because it was convenient. They really needed to have the commitment to come. Why a couple of dozen people? We wanted to ensure that the meeting was manageable and would create an end product. Everyone had to have a chance to be heard and participate fully.

So, while eQualityGiving convened the Dallas meeting, "The Dallas Principles" were created as a joint effort of the two dozen authors, everybody participating and everybody sweating the details to have a great product.

What was the impact of the Dallas Principles?

First, it has become very clear that we were right to push for equality immediately. To the dismay of many LGBT organizations, equality did not flow at the speed that they expected in late 2008 and early 2009. We were making progress, but not in the time frame, quantity, or quality that was expected. Then in 2010, the Democrats lost control of the House as well as many seats in the Senate, and progress come to a standstill (as the Dallas Principles group had predicted).

Second, because of the Dallas Principles, some in the movement adopted the slogan of "Full Equality Now. No Delays. No Excuses." For example, the Human Rights Campaign started a campaign (including T-shirts) with the slogan "No Excuses."

Third, the Dallas Principles became known well beyond the LGBT community. Vice President Biden was made aware of them, as were key White House staffers, key members of Congress, and members of the Democratic National Committee.

Fourth, the Florida LGBT Democratic Caucus adopted the Dallas Principles as their platform for 2012. For the first time in the U.S. history the platform of a major political party (the Democratic party) treats LGBT people in 2012 as fully equal citizens, including the freedom to marry. The Republican party platform of 2012 is similar to the 2008 platform: an insult to LGBT American citizens.

Note that the Green party adopted many years ago a fully pro LGBT equality platform.

Fifth, another positive impact of the Dallas Principles is that there is a growing conversation about *full equality NOW*. However, many still say: I support full LGBT equality now—*but* now is not the time because we do not have a majority in the House, or because President Obama cannot sign an executive order for nondiscrimination during the reelection campaign. So, in reality, these people do not believe in full equality now; they believe in *equality later*.

But as Dr. Martin Luther King Jr. said: "A right delayed is a right denied." How quickly we forget.

So, take your sides: Are you for *equality now* or *equality later*?

If you are for equality now, you can sign up as an endorser of the Dallas Principles at www.ActOnPrinciples.org/endorsers.

The text of the Dallas Principles and information on its authors is listed in appendix 2.

Let's examine next what is needed to have a really inclusive movement for equality.

32.

A Movement for All

For a movement that asks for legal equality for everybody, it is important that we show diversity in all of our efforts. All heads of LGBT organizations believe in diversity. But much more needs to be done to really show that it is a diverse movement.

SEXUAL ORIENTATION DIVERSITY

Too many people are still mistrusting those who self-identify as bisexuals. They think that bisexuals are closeted gays or lesbians. Granted, bisexuals are a minority of the population, and, granted, when they are acting on their opposite gender attraction, they do not suffer the same discrimination as homosexual individuals. But bisexuals are still misunderstood and not represented appropriately in the LGBT movement (including boards of directors).

Furthermore, beyond understanding bisexuals, there are many differences that need to be addressed between gays and lesbians in their approach to giving, politics, and social needs. In summary, many LGBT organizations will benefit from more diversity.

GENDER IDENTITY DIVERSITY

In 2007 the movement got a jolt when Representative Barney Frank said that he will strip transgender protections from his proposed Employment Nondiscrimination Act (ENDA) to enhance the chances of its quick passage. (Five years later, ENDA has not yet passed.) At that time, many prominent LGBT people and the Human Rights Campaign sided with Barney Frank. They said, why not pass protections for gays, lesbians, and bisexuals now and come back later with additional legislation for transgender people? Many others said, we are all in this together. We cannot leave our transgender friends behind. In just a few weeks, more than three hundred LGBT organizations signed up to push for an inclusive

ENDA. A year later Barney Frank reintroduced an inclusive ENDA. Finally, six months later, the Human Rights Campaign supported it.

Since then, in April 2012, the bipartisan Equal Employment Opportunity Commission decided unanimously that transgender people are protected from employment discrimination in Title VII of the Civil Rights Act.

Most LGBT organizations cover transgender people in their programs. However, transgender people are not adequately represented in the governance of organizations in the movement. As of September 2012, the following eighteen national LGBT organizations do not have a single transgender board member:

- Equality Forum

- Family Equality Council

- Freedom to Marry

- Gay and Lesbian Victory Fund

- Gay and Lesbian Leadership Institute

- Ground Spark

- Immigration Equality

- In The Life Media

- Lambda Legal Defense

- Log Cabin Republicans

- Movement Advancement Project

- National Center for Lesbian Rights

- National Stonewall Democrats

- Out & Equal Workplace Advocates

- OutServe

- Servicemembers Legal Defense Network (SLDN)

- Services and Advocacy for Gay, Lesbian, Bisexual and Transgender Elders (SAGE)

- The Trevor Project

Notably, the Human Rights Campaign, the largest LGBT organization, which has a forty-nine-member board, only has one transgender member.

Dr. Dana Beyer, an accomplished transgender advocate, is leading a project of eQualityGiving to increase the number of transgender board members in the governing boards of organizations that represent L+G+B+T people. An up-to-date list of transgender board members is available at: www.eQualityGiving.org/Transgender-Board-Members.

While agreeing on the need of a larger number of transgender board members, executive directors and board chairs provide the following justifications for such lack of representation:

- *It is difficult to find candidates:* This is true; this is why Dr. Beyer's eQualityGiving project includes a list (with bios) of seventeen qualified transgender people who are willing to serve on national boards.

- *It is even more difficult to find candidates that can meet the financial requirements*: This is true, as some of these organizations expect their board members to contribute or fundraise as much as tens of thousands of dollars every year. However, organizations are well served to remember that the primary function of a board is governance, not fundraising (as most like to think). Organizations can always have another board charged with fundraising or waive or reduce fundraising requirements for some board members.

- *They already cover transgender people in their programs:* This is true in most organizations, but it is not a substitute for organizations who claim to represent lesbian, gay, bisexual, and transgender people to have them in their governing board.

RACIAL DIVERSITY

The importance of racial diversity (including on boards) is well understood among LGBT organizations. Progress is occurring, but it still slow. The experiences and needs of white, African-American, Latino, Asian, or Native American LGBT Americans are different.

POLITICAL DIVERSITY

About 75 percent of LGBT Americans vote for democrats. This is one of the most solid and consistent voting blocks for the Democratic party. Yet, this party did not bring to a vote the Employment Nondiscrimination Act in 2009–10 while the party had the majority in the House and Senate.

It is important to acknowledge that a minority of LGBT people are Republicans. It is critical to ensure that legislators understand that LGBT equality is a nonpartisan issue. The Log Cabin Republicans work with the minority of Republican legislators who support some LGBT rights. The majority of Republican legislators in Congress are strongly anti-equality. This is evidenced by their party platform, as well as by their votes against federal hate-crime legislation and repeal of Don't Ask, Don't Tell.

Given their mission and charter, Log Cabin Republicans cannot endorse a Democratic candidate. They were wise, however, not to endorse George W. Bush for reelection in 2004. In 2008, they endorsed John McCain and ran advertisements in the primary forcefully opposing Mitt Romney. It will be interesting to see if they endorse Romney/Ryan this time—and, if they do, what rationale they present.

33.

Summary: Equal Under the Law

A main foundation of American society is the belief that everybody should be treated equally under the law. This is same belief that is the essence of the Gay Agenda: to be treated equally under the law.

Here are the areas of the law in which heterosexual, homosexual, bisexual, and transgender Americans are not yet treated the same under most states' laws and federal law:

- *Hate crimes legislation.* Covered at the federal level, but not covered in most states.

- *Nondiscrimination in employment, housing, credit, public accommodation and facilities, and federally funded programs or activities.* Not treated equally at the federal level, or in most states.

- *Serving in the military without lying about who you are* (achieved) and *not being discriminated due to your sexual orientation and gender identity* (not achieved yet).

- *Marrying the person you love and having the freedom to live anywhere in the United States as a married couple.* Not achieved yet.

- *Free to match your biological gender to your true gender.* Partially achieved.

- *A safe environment for all youth* to learn without bullying and harassment. Not achieved at the federal level, or in most states.

- *Being able to be a parent and raise a family like everybody else.* Need federal legislation and additional legislation in most states.

What paths can we take to be better and treat everybody equally under the law? The next chapter has some suggestions.

Part III:

Different Paths?

34.

Three Main Paths

There are three main paths to reach legal equality:

1. Courts
2. Legislatures
3. Popular vote

These are the same paths that have led us to lose equality. Opponents of LGBT equality are using the same methods used in the past to deny equality to other groups. Just a few decades ago, the preferred method to oppose equality was to pass legislation to marginalize, or even criminalize, any group that opponents of equality did not like (e.g. African Americans or gays or women). Another preferred method is to call for the "right of the people to vote" to amend state or federal constitutions to take rights away (e.g., prohibition of alcohol, marriage equality). They would convince people to vote their way—many times through emotional, but false, appeals to "save the children." When the courts would grant equality, as required by the constitution, then opponents would label the judges as "activists" and seek to overturn their rulings by popular vote and even recall or impeach the judges.

In the past, in their disdain for some groups, such as African Americans, opponents of equal rights went much further by going into a civil war and endangering the whole existence of our incipient nation. Many of these citizens who proclaimed to be for law and order would openly disregard court orders, such as for school integration. Or, worse yet, these citizens would take justice in their own hands, sometimes as part of supremacist organizations.

Fortunately, things are better now. We are not waging civil wars to solve our problems, but the willingness to keep rights and protections only for the majority continues.

As a country, we are better than that. In the next chapter, let's review how the courts, the legislatures, and popular vote can be used to bring equality under the law to *all* Americans.

35.

Path #1: The Courts

In their brilliancy, the Founding Fathers established a government system based on three *independent* branches. This independence among the branches is critical, especially for the legal rights of minorities. It is possible, but difficult, for minorities to get equal rights via legislation. This is because legislators, by the reason of being elected by the majority, look first at legislation that affects the majority. They also may feel the pressure from the majority to legislate to marginalize unpopular minorities—such as legislating what consenting adults can or cannot do in the privacy of their bedroom or legislating against interracial marriage.

This is why the role of the courts is to be an independent branch that is not focused on the wishes of the majority but rather on the constitution. One of the most important Supreme Court decisions for treating LGBT people equally was *Lawrence v Texas*, which in 2003 struck down all the sodomy laws, which also applied to heterosexuals. This was important, because some people say that they do not oppose gays, just what they do in bed. Who are they to assume, much less judge, what consenting adults do in the privacy of their bedroom?

Here is what the US Supreme Court had to say in its majority decision in *Lawrence v Texas*:

> Liberty presumes an autonomy of self that includes freedom of thought, belief, expression, and certain intimate conduct.

> When sexuality finds overt expression in intimate conduct with another person, the conduct can be but one element in a personal bond that is more enduring. The liberty protected by the Constitution allows homosexual persons the right to make this choice.

> When homosexual conduct is made criminal by the law of the State, that declaration in and of itself is an invitation to subject *homosexual persons to discrimination both in the public and in the private spheres.*

In another important judicial decision, in 2004 the Massachusetts Supreme Judicial Court in *Goodridge v. Department of Public Health* acknowledged that there are different points of view regarding same-gender marriage:

> Many people hold deep-seated religious, moral, and ethical convictions that marriage should be limited to the union of one man and one woman, and that homosexual conduct is immoral. Many hold equally strong religious, moral, and ethical convictions that same-sex couples are entitled to be married, and that homosexual persons should be treated no differently than their heterosexual neighbors.

But in the end it comes down to individual autonomy and equality under the law. The court continued:

> Marriage is a vital social institution.

> A person who enters into an intimate, exclusive union with another of the same sex is arbitrarily deprived of membership in one of our community's most rewarding and cherished institutions. That exclusion is incompatible with the constitutional principles of respect for individual autonomy and equality under law.

So the courts acknowledge that there are differences of opinion—but show that *the respect for individual autonomy and equality under the law should trump anything else.* That is the key principle that unites all us Americans. Still, some say the ruling is wrong, that they are "activist" judges, creating laws instead of just interpreting them. The next chapter carefully examines this concern.

36.

Activist Judges

Some people complain about judicial activism, which popularly means that judges "legislate from the bench." These people believe that judges are taking the power from the people's representatives to create new laws and rights where none exist in the constitution.

Some people would like the U.S. Constitution to be read literally, as it was written more than two hundred years ago. The reality is that the world has changed in the last two centuries. For instance, the role of the president as commander-in-chief also applies to the Air Force, despite that an Air Force is never mentioned in the constitution. Also, fortunately, we no longer consider that someone is three-fifths of a person.

Most people complaining about activist judges are conservatives. This criticism is usually addressed from the right to judges who have supported the freedom of individuals to marry the person they love. The reality is that studies show that the U.S. Supreme Court, headed by conservative John Roberts, has been the most "activist" in decades, including the controversial ruling in *Citizens United v. Federal Election Commission* (January 21, 2010) in which the Supreme Court ruled that Congress could not impose limits to financial contributions from corporations and unions. This was an expansion well beyond what the Constitution says (which is mute about the subject) and well beyond established precedents.

In fact, in *Citizen's United*, the Supreme Court went well beyond the outcome the plaintiff was asking. This is extreme activism. Citizen's United, represented by Ted Olson (who represented Bush in 2000 and won the presidency for him) only wanted a ruling that said that long movies showed on a pay-per-view channel did not constitute electioneering and should be allowed to be shown before an election. Olson specifically asked the court not to change precedent about campaign finance legislation. Breaking precedent, restraint, and moderation, the Supreme Court completely changed the financing of elections—this will make it much, much harder for

Democrats to win in 2012 at all levels of government. (Check the article *Money Unlimited* by Jeffrey Toobin in the *New Yorker*, May 21, 2012.)

Some politicians, such as Newt Gingrich, have gone as far as to state that the president should send the police to arrest a judge in order to compel appearance in front of a Congressional committee to justify his or her rulings (on MSNBC's *Face the Nation*, December 18, 2011). Mr. Gingrich's demand is an attack on American democracy.

American democracy is based on three *independent* branches of government. The president (executive branch) cannot order anybody to appear in front of Congress (legislative branch). Similarly, Congress cannot compel judges (judicial branch) to reverse their rulings. Certainly, Congress can create new laws that, if they are constitutional, can have the effect of reversing a ruling. What a sad state of affairs, when a politician makes such an outrageous statement and tries to undermine our democracy so heavily.

When we use the term *activist judges*, we are in reality attacking the independence of the three branches of government. As we said before, the brilliance of the American democracy is the separation of powers. Legislators, elected by majority, tend to write legislation that represents the interest of the majority that elected them. Sometimes this legislation unnecessarily hurts a minority. This is why we need the judicial branch that, at the federal level, is not subject to elections, to ensure that the rights of the minority are protected. We should all agree to support the *key constitutional principle of independence of judges*.

Fortunately, more and more legislators are seeing the fairness of creating legislation that treats everybody equally under the law, and they are approving, for instance, legislation that grants civil marriage licenses to couples independently of their gender. Read on for further discussion of the role of the legislatures for equality.

37.

Path #2: The Legislatures

To have legislation enacted that treat minorities equally under the law, we need to

1. Support the election (and reelection) of legislators who are pro-equality. We need to support these candidates independently of their party affiliation (although most are Democrats) and their sexual orientation (many of our biggest supporters are heterosexual).

2. Follow up after the election to ensure that these legislators introduce and support pro-equality legislation.

3. Convince other legislators to vote for equality legislation. The more they get to know gay, lesbian, bisexual, and transgender constituents, the more they understand their personal plight due to discrimination, and the more than they support pro-equality legislation.

The next four chapters present practical approaches regarding legislative activism.

38.

Endorsing Candidates for Elected Office

Multiple organizations endorse candidates. For example, the Victory Fund only endorse candidates who are lesbian, gay, bisexual, or transgender. This is a good long-term strategy. Clearly, having LGBT elected officials helps their colleagues understand the humanity of their vote and has been effective in passing equality legislation. However, there are heterosexual legislators who have been more supportive on equality issues than their LGBT counterparts.

Another organization, Log Cabin Republicans, supports only Republican candidates, but, contrary to the Victory Fund, they endorse independently of sexual orientation. Their pickings are slim. So, most times they endorse candidates who are partly pro-equality.

To reach equality under the law, we need to endorse and elect candidates who are fully pro-equality, independently of their party affiliation or sexual orientation or gender identity or expression. While party affiliation makes a difference in terms of which party has a majority, it is beneficial to have pro-equality legislators in each party. And while it is good to have legislators who are LGBT, heterosexual legislators are vital to getting bills passed.

Volunteers and donors do not need to compromise anymore: *Support with your money and time only those candidates who are publicly and fully pro-equality, including marriage equality.*

eQualityGiving, the organization that my partner and I founded in 2005, endorses candidates who support all the Equality Goals—independently of party affiliation or sexual orientation. Here is how candidates are categorized:

- *Pro-Equality candidates:* they support *all* the Equality Goals.

If they are in a competitive race (up to ten points from opponent), they are considered *Endorsed Candidates to Fund.*

If they are not in a competitive race (for instance, leading by more than ten points, or lagging the competitor by more than ten points), they are considered *Endorsed Candidates.* You can give to them if you have a good reason, such as knowing them personally, but in general it is better to explain that you will support them when they are in a close race. In the meantime it is more strategic for you to fund pro-equality candidates in competitive races.

- *Co-endorsed candidates.* This is the situation in which multiple candidates are pro-equality in the same race. You may choose to support one of the candidates for other reasons such as party affiliation, sexual orientation, experience, gender, their position on other issues, etc. Otherwise it is best to reserve the money to support the winner in the general election or invest your money elsewhere if both candidates in the general are pro-equality.

- *Heartbreakers.* These are candidates in favor of most but not all of the Equality Goals or who claim that they cannot be public with their full support for equality. The strategy is to encourage them to become pro-equality and not fund them or volunteer for them until they do so. In 2012 *we are past the point of supporting Heartbreakers;* with so many pro-equality candidates to support, we need to focus only on those who have already evolved to be fully pro-equality.

- *Candidates to defeat.* These are candidates who are anti-equality because of their positions or actions (for example, by vetoing pro-equality legislation or supporting anti-equality constitutional amendments).

Most endorsement lists limit themselves to endorsed candidates. We need more detailed categories like those shown above. For example, it is important to endorse, but not fund, somebody who is pro-equality and has a big lead in the polls. Similarly, a race might be a Heartbreaker vs. a Candidate to Defeat. While you may not want to support wholeheartedly a candidate who does not support us fully, you may want to work hard to defeat the opponent, especially if it is an anti-equality candidate.

eQualityGiving's list of Endorsed and co-endorsed Candidates is available here: www.eQualityGiving.org/Endorsed-Candidates.

What if somebody asks you to support an incumbent member of Congress who is not listed by eQualityGiving as an Endorsed Candidate? With 535 members of Congress, it is possible that they were overlooked. But more than likely, it is possible that the person is not fully pro-equality. There are two complementary ways to check:

- First, check whether they are co-sponsoring all the major equality bills. The most effective way to check on this is going to ActOnPrinciples.org (which I also founded).

- Second, check their score on the Human Rights Campaign's scorecard (hrc.org). It indicates how they voted on issues. Although that scoring system has some flaws, in general you only want to support candidates with a 100 percent score.

An argument given for supporting candidates who may not be fully pro-equality is that it makes a difference which party has majorities in Congress and the State legislatures. This is a valid argument. While we may need bipartisan support to pass equality legislation, the reality is that the vast majority of Democratic elected officials support equality, while the vast majority of Republican elected officials oppose it. Furthermore, Republicans are highly unlikely to bring pro-equality legislation for a vote (although a few of them would vote for it). So it may seem logical to give money to the Democratic party to ensure that majority. In reality, it is best to support pro-equality candidates directly. You keep control. At the same time it frees money from the party to support other candidates to reach the majority they desire.

You will also hear the argument in favor of giving money to a party to ensure a higher turnout of voters. You can do this if you wish, but check other organizations beforehand that can be as effective or more to turn out the vote.

Another issue is whether to co-endorse candidates. If an organization has clear criteria for endorsement (such as support for all Equality Goals), then co-endorsements are necessary to provide the full picture to donors and volunteers. Take a poignant example: a race in which two candidates support our full legal equality. One of the candidates is LGBT. Which one do you support? If your endorsement criteria call for endorsing only LGBT candidates, then it makes sense to endorse only the LGBT candidate. However, you need to disclose to the donors and volunteers that the opponent is also fully pro-equality. Some donors and volunteers still will pour their support for the LGBT candidate, but other donors and volunteers may prefer to spend their efforts in another race in which their support can increase the total number of elected officials who support our equality.

Here is a list of the basic endorsement principles:

- *Support only candidates that are fully and publicly pro-equality,* as evidenced by the candidate signing a questionnaire. If they are not on the record (through a public questionnaire or public statements), don't support them (even if they tell you that they will support you once elected, or that they understand our issues because they have an LGBT family member or friend).

- *Support candidates at all levels:* for president, for Congress, for statewide office, for State Assembly and Senate, for town council and mayors, for school boards (which are influential in determining what is taught at schools and anti-bullying policies), for police boards (to ensure that our community is treated equally), and for judges (very important endorsements but often neglected).

- *Support candidates independently of sexual orientation.* In a race between two pro-equality candidates, it is best to invest in a different race (so as to increase the total number of pro-equality candidates). But everything being equal, it is usually best to invest in openly LGBT candidates.

- *Support candidates independently of party affiliation* (if you can accept their positions on other issues important to you). Even if you invest only in Republican candidates, invest only in those who are completely pro-equality (including marriage).

- *Do not support Heartbreakers.* Instead encourage them to become fully pro-equality (and then give them your support).

- *Support specific candidates instead of giving money to a party as discussed earlier.*

- *Support organizations that are trying to ensure that our elections are verifiable and auditable.* This is critical.

- *Support pro-equality organizations that are trying to register people and get out the vote.* Ensure that these organizations fully support the issue of equality and periodically motivate their members to lobby Congress and state legislators for full equality.

If you decide to give to candidates based on a list from an endorsing organization, verify the following:

- What are the endorsing criteria?
- Are the endorsing criteria public?
- Do the criteria differentiate among candidates who are fully pro-equality and those who are not?
- Do the criteria require candidates to be public about their positions on LGBT equality?
- Do the criteria differentiate among candidates who need funding and those who don't (either because they are almost guaranteed to win, or have only a slim chance to win)?
- Do the criteria allow for co-endorsements? This is critical information so that you can allocate your resources, if you choose, to another race.

A cautionary note: some endorsing organizations like to mention their win rate (i.e. how many endorsed candidates win). The win rate is *not* really meaningful—any organization can reach a high win rate—it is a matter of how safe it wants to select the candidates.

As you can imagine, when founding eQualityGiving, we put lots of thought on the endorsement process. eQualityGiving fulfills all the criteria listed above. Its endorsements are nonpartisan and irrespective of sexual orientation/gender identity/expression (but both are disclosed). Currently we endorse only federal (president, Congress) and statewide (governors, attorneys general) elections.

In addition to eQualityGiving, other organizations also prepare endorsements. Most notably:

- Gill Action, which endorses in state races. It is funded through the generosity of software entrepreneur and philanthropist Tim Gill. Mostly, they do not make their endorsement list public. For more information, check www.GillAction.org.

- Victory Fund, which does campaign training in addition to endorsements exclusively for LGBT candidates. They do not disclose their endorsement criteria, or whether or not there are other pro-equality candidates in the race. More information can be found at www.VictoryFund.org.

- Human Rights Campaign. The endorsement criteria are not made public. More information is available at www.HRC.org. HRC often endorses candidates with huge leads in the polls.

- Stonewall Democrats, which only endorses Democratic candidates. More information is at their website, www.StonewallDemocrats.org.

- Log Cabin Republicans, which only endorses Republican candidates. More information is at www.LogCabin.org.

- LPAC, a new lesbian super PAC. More information at www.teamlpac.com.

To win equality, we need to support pro-equality candidates—but all the money invested does not matter if the votes are not counted accurately. We are still not very good at counting votes, as the next chapter discusses.

39.

Counting the Votes

In November 2000, Americans learned a very important lesson about the most fundamental right in a democracy: the ability to accurately and verifiably determine who the people have voted for and thus chosen to represent them.

The events of the November 2000 presidential election illustrated a series of problems:

- Unreliable machines that left punch cards with hanging chads
- Butterfly ballots that confused voters
- Bullies banging on the doors of the recount office, intimidating and forcing others to stop the recount
- The limitations of the electoral college as a way to choose a president
- The fact that the presidential election was not decided by 537 votes in Florida, but by just one vote in the Supreme Court

The 2000 presidential election showed that each vote makes a difference. What has happened then in the last twelve years to improve our elections?

In October 2002, by a bipartisan vote, Congress approved the Help America Vote Act (HAVA). This legislation has a very significant flaw: it funded the elimination of punch-card and lever machines while recommending that they be replaced by Direct Recording Electronic (DRE) voting machines that cannot be audited. The good news is that there will be no more hanging chads; the bad news is that, wherever paperless DREs are used, there is no way now to verify the voter's intentions.

In early 2005, the Democratic National Committee established a commission (of which I was appointed as a member) to analyze whether there was fraud in Ohio in the presidential election in November 2004. My research discovered the solution to one of the biggest problems in an election: how to audit the aggregation of the results from each voting station to form the final count for a district or a state. My solution got lots of attention and were codified into legislation introduced by Dr. Rush Holt, a physicist, who is a member of Congress representing the Princeton area and who is the foremost expert in Congress on election law.

Congressman Rush Holt has introduced multiple times a number of bills pertaining specifically to protecting the accuracy, integrity and security of the vote count. His Voter Confidence and Increased Accessibility Act (introduced first in 2003) would have established requirements and provided funding for verifiable elections through the use of paper ballots and routine random audits. Similarly with his Emergency Assistance for Secure Elections Act (introduced in 2008). Two additional pieces of legislation, the Vote Tabulation Audit Act (introduced first in 2006) and the Poll Tape Transparency Act (introduced first in 2008), both based on my ideas, would have provided for transparent and verifiable aggregation of vote tallies.

Although all of these pieces of legislation have been pending in several successive Congresses, only the Voter Confidence and Increased Accessibility Act and the Emergency Assistance for Secure Elections Act were ever reported by Committee, and only the Emergency Assistance for Secure Elections Act ever received a floor vote. It did receive a majority of support, but it was brought to the floor under a procedural rule requiring a supermajority. The Bush Administration circulated a statement of policy against the legislation in advance of the vote, and it failed to receive the supermajority required. Neither bill was again brought to the floor, even though various versions of each had earned a majority of support in the House. This has been a big failure on the part of the Democratic Party.

Meanwhile, the Republican Party has been very proactive and successful in passing legislation in several states to make it more difficult for voters to register to vote or to vote if they are already registered. They claim that the purpose of the legislation is to ensure that only citizens vote—but this is false, since the level of fraud of non citizens voting is extremely small (for example in a lawsuit in Pennsylvania, the state could not show a single case of non-citizens voting). The real aim of that legislation is to make it more difficult for certain groups of citizens to vote: seniors, minorities, poor people, and college students. These are groups that tend to vote much more Democratic than Republican.

This information is very relevant if you are involved in establishing equality through the legislature. You may support the proper candidates, but if we cannot verify that there were no errors in the vote count, and if we cannot ensure that all eligible voters will be able to register and vote without being blocked by disenfranchising barriers, all of our efforts may be for naught. So, if you are investing heavily in politics, either with your money or your time, you should consider supporting legislation at the state and federal levels to ensure the auditability and audit of elections, and unobstructed voter registration and voting.

The best report on voting machine auditability and preparedness is *Counting Votes 2012: A State by State Look at Voting Technology Preparedness*, which is available for a free download at www.countingvotes.org. The best reports on the recent changes to voter registration and voter identification laws are *Voting Law Changes in 2012*, *The Challenge of Obtaining Voter Identification*, and *State Restrictions on Voter Registration Drives*, which are available for free download at www.brennancenter.org

Good organizations working on this include the following:

- Verified Voting (www.verifiedvoting.org)

- Brennan Center for Justice at New York University Law School (www.brennancenter.org)

- Common Cause Education Fund (www.commoncause.org)

- Advancement Project (www.advancementproject.org)

- Election Protection Coalition (www.866ourvote.org)

In 2000 counting the votes became all-important thanks to an activist Supreme Court, which decided the presidential election by one vote. In 2012 counting the money will be all-important thanks to an activist Supreme Court, which changed the role of money in elections by one vote. The next chapter further investigates money's role in elections.

40.

Counting the Money

Money has always played a role in politics. In 2010, the US Supreme Court ruled in a 5 to 4 decision that corporations and unions can spend unlimited amounts of money on political electioneering communications, including advocating for the election or defeat of candidates (*Citizens United v. Federal Election Commission*). The conservative majority of the Supreme Court also decided that such unlimited expenditures do not constitute "a risk of corruption or the appearance of corruption."

Who are they kidding?

Justice Stevens in his dissent said,

> At bottom, the Court's opinion is thus a rejection of the common sense of the American people, who have recognized a need to prevent corporations from undermining self government since the founding, and who have fought against the distinctive corrupting potential of corporate electioneering since the days of Theodore Roosevelt.

This was a major activist decision, breaking precedent, and not giving due deference to Congress (which had imposed limitations on such expenditures). This is exactly the opposite to the restraint that Chief Justice Roberts claimed during his confirmation hearings.

But it gets worse: Two months after that decision, the Federal Court of Appeals for the D.C. Circuit ruled on the case of *Speechnow.org v. FEC*.

The end result of both decisions is the creation a new entity: Super PACs, which can raise *unlimited amounts of money* from corporations, unions, other groups and individuals, and they do *not* need to disclose the identity of the donors. They have some trivial limitations: they cannot coordinate with a campaign and cannot make direct financial contributions to campaigns. But they can pay for their own advertisements even targeting specific candidates.

This is not democracy for the people and by the people. Unfortunately, the only solution to this is an amendment to the constitution, which is very difficult. One of the organizations working on this is FreeSpeechForPeople.org.

The next chapter focuses on passing legislation after elections.

41.

From Endorsements to Legislation: Act on Principles

Endorsing candidates who are pro-equality is critical for achieving equality under the law. Then we have to ensure that they win despite unlimited and secret financing and despite that, in most states, there is no way to audit the results of the election because of the use of electronic voting machines with no verifiable paper trail.

If a pro-equality candidate wins, despite all of these obstacles, it is time to get into action—we need to ensure that pro-equality legislators actually introduce legislation that will bring full legal equality to all Americans. To do so, there is a powerful new internet tool: Act On Principles (www.ActOnPrinciples.org), which lists all the federal pro-equality legislation that has been introduced in Congress and identifies how each member of Congress is expected to vote on it. This tool also allows any interested party to update the vote count with any new information. Furthermore, webmasters can insert in their sites a widget that keeps the up-to-the minute vote count.

All parties in Congress and state legislatures, use Whip Counts, which is asking the members of their party how they plan to vote on a piece of legislation. This helps the party leadership determine what to introduce for a vote. Lobbyists also keep their own, private whip counts (covering both parties) to determine candidates that need to be convinced for a given vote. Whip counts have always been a very closely guarded secret. This new tool makes whip counts open and transparent—quite a revolution. This tool was created and is funded by me; Donald Hitchcock maintains the website; Lane Hudson and John Bare serve as editors.

In the last few chapters, we have talked about achieving legal equality through legislation. But what about losing rights by popular vote? Isn't voting the essence of democracy? The next chapter addresses these crucial questions and more.

42.

Path #3: Popular Vote

This is a democracy; let's all vote!

Certainly, voting is a critical part of a democracy. But should we vote on fundamental rights? How would you like if people had a vote on whether *you* have the right to marry? Let's take the case that the person you love is from a different race. Should you have the right to marry? Should we take a vote on this?

In 1967, when the Supreme Court decided that interracial marriage should be legal, 72 percent of Americans were opposed to it (source: www.religioustolerance.org/hom_mar14.htm)

In November 2000, there was a vote in Alabama to eliminate from their statutes the prohibition against interracial marriage. Only 60 percent of voters in Alabama agreed to that removal, despite that in the whole United States it had been illegal to forbid interracial marriage for thirty-three years.

As recently as in March 2011, a poll of Republicans voters in Mississippi revealed that 46 percent of them believe that you should not have the right to marry somebody of a different race (source: www.religioustolerance.org/hom_mar14.htm).

So, was it an activist Supreme Court that allowed interracial marriages? After all, while the Constitution is silent about interracial marriages (as it is about gay marriage), clearly when the Constitution was enacted, interracial marriage was forbidden in most states. Fortunately, the Supreme Court in 1967 saw their job as being *independent*. They understood that even if a very large majority of Americans were opposed to interracial marriage, you cannot deny the fundamental right of a person to marry the person they love. Also fortunately, we did not take it for a vote in 1967 about whether interracial marriage should be legal. Clearly it would have lost. The lesson, of course, is that we *cannot put the rights of a minority to a majority vote.*

We have examined so far the three main paths to win (or lose) equality: the courts, the legislatures, and the popular vote. The next chapter will examine other strategies that apply to each of these three main paths.

43.

State or Federal Paths?

Should we reach equality by going state by state or by getting federal rights?

The answer is that it depends on the Equality Goal and the composition of the legislature of a given state versus Congress. So let's examine them one goal at a time:

EQUALITY GOAL: HATE CRIMES—DONE FEDERALLY— WORK NEEDED IN STATES

A great achievement of the Obama presidency and Congress was to pass the Matthew Shepard and James Byrd Jr. Hate Crimes Prevention Act in 2009 when the Democratic party held the majority. This legislation is very useful, but it is not a replacement for hate-crimes legislation in the states. Only fourteen states and the District of Columbia have hate-crime legislation that cover sexual orientation and gender identity and expression. Several states can be added if we focus our efforts. In a few states, it may take much longer since they have Republican majorities which are usually not willing to bring equality legislation for a vote.

EQUALITY GOAL: NONDISCRIMINATION NEEDS TO BE DONE FEDERALLY AND IN THE MAJORITY OF STATES

This has been an elusive goal to achieve, despite that it is supported by most Americans and that it is fundamental for every person's well-being. The Employment Nondiscrimination Act had enough votes to pass Congress in 2010, but it was not put for a vote. Furthermore, in twenty-nine states, there is no protection for nondiscrimination in employment, credit, housing, and public accommodation based on sexual orientation and gender identity and expression. Obviously, there is a great deal of work to do at the federal and state levels.

EQUALITY GOAL: SERVING IN THE MILITARY— PARTLY ACCOMPLISHED

The Don't Ask, Don't Tell Act was repealed in 2011. This was a great victory again for the Obama presidency, and the repeal passed Congress with overwhelming Democratic support and the support of a handful of fair-minded Republicans.

The legislation, while allowing service members to be open about their sexuality, does not protect them against discrimination. Before the repeal, you were fired from the military just for disclosing that you were gay (or from somebody saying you were). Now you cannot be fired for disclosing it, but if you are fired and suspect that was exclusively because of homophobia, you have no real recourse. There is still work to do on this federal goal. At the state level, there is not much work to do for this goal, since most of the national guards follow the Department of Defense policies.

EQUALITY GOAL: MARRIAGE EQUALITY—LOTS OF WORK AT STATE AND FEDERAL LEVEL

Civil marriage licenses are issued at the state level. At this time, the freedom to marry any person you love is available in only six states (Connecticut, Iowa, Massachusetts, New Hampshire, New York, and Vermont) and the District of Columbia. However, these marriages are not recognized by the federal government.

In three states (Maine, Maryland, and Washington) marriage equality will be on the ballot on November 2012. In one state (California), the issue is under litigation, and has won so far in the California Supreme Court, in federal court, and in the federal court of appeals. It is now headed to the US Supreme Court. If it takes the case, it will be decided next year; if it declines to take the case, same-gender marriage will be legal in California again.

So, there is much work to be done—but only a handful of states are potential candidates (either because they already have civil unions that could be converted to marriage or because they have no constitutional amendment forbidding same-gender marriage). The vast majority of states have constitutional amendments, so the state path to marriage is basically closed in those states.

Although issuing civil marriage licenses is a state issue, federal legislation and litigation are critical for two main reasons: First, the Defense of Marriage Act (DOMA) does not allow recognition of those marriages at the federal level. This is overt discrimination. Imagine that you are a different-gender couple legally married in a state, and the federal government treats you as unmarried. It complicates your everyday life. President Obama and the Department of Justice determined that DOMA is unconstitutional, and therefore they are not supporting it in any litigation (although they are still enforcing it until a court overturns it or it is repealed by Congress). In the meantime, the Republicans in the House of Representatives have authorized millions of tax dollars to be used to hire private attorneys to litigate the case for them.

Second, if you are married in a state, your marriage needs to be recognized in the other states (even if they do not issue marriage licenses to same-gender couples). Imagine the nightmare: you are married and traveling and have an accident and in that state they say that you are a legal stranger to your spouse since they do not recognize your marriage!

So, there is much work to be done at both the state and federal levels.

EQUALITY GOAL: FREEDOM OF GENDER—LOTS OF WORK NEEDED MOSTLY IN THE STATES

Thanks to a unanimous ruling of the Equal Opportunity Commission, transgender people are now protected against employment discrimination under Title VII of the Civil Rights Act. This is a tremendous victory at the federal level. In addition, thanks to several policies enacted by the Obama administration, transgender individuals are treated more equally by federal policies. The most notable need at the federal level is to modify uniform and medical policies so that transgender people can serve openly in the military. At the state level, however, there is much work to be done, particularly regarding birth certificates, driver's licenses, and insurance coverage.

EQUALITY GOAL: PROTECTING YOUTH—LOTS OF WORK NEEDED AT FEDERAL AND STATE LEVELS

Education is mostly a state issue. With only eighteen states protecting youth against bullying because of sexual orientation or gender identity or expression, there is much work to be done. At the federal level, three anti-bullying bills have been proposed covering bullying at different levels of schooling. These federal bills need to be integrated into one and enacted by Congress.

EQUALITY GOAL: PARENTING—WORK NEEDED AT STATE AND FEDERAL LEVELS

Parenting is mostly a state issue, and, in the vast majority of states, LGBT individuals or couples can adopt—although the statutes are not uniform and in many cases depend on the jurisdiction within a state. At the federal level Senator Kirsten Gillibrand (D-NY) has introduced an adoption law, and it needs to pass Congress.

Now that we have a better understanding of which Equality Goals need more state or federal legislation, in the next chapter let's talk about winning hearts and minds.

44.

Winning Hearts and Minds

Whether you follow the path of the courts, or the legislatures, or popular votes, a key component for each of them is to win hearts and minds of the American people. Popular TV shows and movies have helped Americans understand better that there are lesbian, gay, bisexual, and transgender individuals in all walks of life and that, at the end of the day, we are all basically the same—we are all human beings with our accomplishments, strengths, weaknesses, and needs.

If you are an LGBT person in the closet, the most effective step that you can take to win hearts and minds is to come out to friends, family, coworkers, and basically everybody. Most people will be very accepting and embracing. Most of your friends and family may already suspect anyway.

Organizations also work hard to change hearts and minds, the most well known being GLAAD (glaad.org).

45.

Equal Rights and Businesses

While awaiting federal and state legislation to provide nondiscrimination, we need to rely on policies adopted voluntarily by businesses. Since 2002, the Human Rights Campaign provides a Corporate Equality Index. Appendix 3 lists companies to which the Human Rights Campaign has given a 100 percent rating in the Corporate Equality Index. This index shows tremendous progress by American corporations: eighty-eight of the top 500 Fortune corporations have a perfect rating of 100 percent, and ten of the top twenty corporations in America reach the same perfect rating. But legislation to protect against nondiscrimination is badly needed since the Fortune 500 covers only a small proportion of employment in the United States.

Note that an executive order from the president requiring that all federal contractors do not discriminate in employment based on sexual orientation or gender identity or expression would immediately cover almost twenty percent of the working population in the United States. Such an executive order is ready for President Obama's signature. He has indicated that he will not signed it until after the election.

A new issue has surfaced after the Citizens United decision by the Supreme Court in 2010: Corporations can donate *unlimited* amounts of money for electioneering. And they can do so *anonymously*. So a corporation may be giving to elect conservative candidates to get them to lower their corporate taxes and reduce regulation. Given that most fiscally conservative candidates are nowadays also socially conservative, the corporations may be giving to candidates who legislate against equality. A corporation may even have a 100 percent rating in the Corporate Equality Index and may even donate to an LGBT nonprofit—while at the same time supporting candidates who are anti-equality.

To solve this problem requires external pressure as well as inside advocates (in which OutAndEqual.org and employee LGBT groups play a key role). This represents one of the most important and unresolved issues facing our relationship with corporations. It is also a difficult problem to resolve because corporate giving for electioneering can be impossible to track since it can be done anonymously.

46.

Building Coalitions

Not to state the obvious, but work to reach equality requires building coalitions; these coalitions need to

- show businesses that LGBT customers and others are loyal customers to corporations that support basic principles like equality;

- demonstrate every day to employers that LGBT employees perform excellently in their jobs;

- demonstrate to the African-American community that the LGBT community truly understands their issues, their culture, and their religious heritage, and that our organizations are truly diverse;

- help the immigrant communities that, like LGBT people, want to be full US citizens and not second class.

- continue supporting the disability community, as they have supported the LGBT community.

- have governing boards for LGBT organizations composed of gay and lesbian and bisexual and transgender board members.

The following chapter reviews what we've learned in Part III.

47.

Summary: The Paths to Equality

We have seen that there are three main paths to legal equality:

1. *Courts*
   This is the most cost effective way. We discussed the real meaning of activist judges and why the current conservative Supreme Court is very much activist.

2. *Legislatures*
   It is key to have a high-quality and transparent process for endorsing candidates and then follow up after the election to ensure that legislation is introduced, supported, and passed.

3. *Popular Vote*
   Putting the rights of a minority up to a vote of the majority is clearly the easiest way to lose equality instead of achieving it.

Then we presented, for each of the Equality Goals, the work that needs to be done at the federal and state level.

We discussed the newest issue in our relationships with businesses: some companies are very good with LGBT employees and customers while at the same time helping elect anti-equality legislators who will have a detrimental impact on our rights.

Finally, for any of the main paths to equality, we need to continue winning hearts and minds and building coalitions.

We have examined formal paths to equality. In the next chapters we'll explore what path *you* can take to make a difference.

Part IV:

Your Turn

48.

Acting Differently

Here's to the crazy ones, the misfits, the rebels, the troublemakers, the round pegs in the square holes... because the people who are crazy enough to think that they can change the world are the ones that do.

—Original text for the first "Think different" Apple
commercial, 1997;
narrated by Steve Jobs

An important way to accelerate reaching equality is by *acting differently*: pushing the envelope and creating new ideas and approaches, because many times progress comes from unexpected sources. Below are some "Going" stories that highlight Acting Differently.

GOING TO THE STREETS

November 4, 2008 was a sad day for equal rights: A referendum in California took away the right to marry in that state. Eighteen thousand same-gender couples were married in the six months while it was legal. Fortunately, these marriages were not voided. But this created three classes of citizens in California:

1. those who could marry (and remarry) as they wish;
2. those who could not marry; and
3. those who were married but could not remarry.

Just two weeks after that vote, there were demonstrations all around the country in support of marriage equality. Who organized these demonstrations? The big LGBT organizations? No, just two people out of Seattle with a computer and much passion and creativity—an example of Acting Differently, and boldly.

GOING TO THE SUPREME COURT

The legal organizations working for LGBT equality have done an outstanding job securing more and more victories in the courts, including the critical 2003 victory of *Lawrence v Texas* in the Supreme Court, which decriminalized homosexuality.

Regarding the right to marry, the LGBT legal organizations have been building the case very carefully and wanted all their ducks in a row before going to the U.S. Supreme Court. All of this changed in 2009 when Chad Griffin, a non-lawyer with significant contacts in Hollywood, asked himself, why not bring a marriage case to the Supreme Court now? Of course, very aware of the risks, he then said, what if we go to the Supreme Court with the dream team of lawyers?

There are a couple of attorneys that come to everybody's mind when being represented in front of the Supreme Court: Ted Olson, a conservative, who represented George W. Bush in *Bush v Gore*, the lawsuit in 2000 that decided the campaign for the most important job on the planet; and David Boies, a liberal with extensive Supreme Court experience, who represented Al Gore on the same case. What if you could have a conservative and a liberal, Olson and Boies, both on the same side and representing the freedom to marry in front of the Supreme Court? This would be a dream come true! Well, Chad Griffin made it happen (although his approach was considered controversial and risky by many heads of equality organizations). Chad then founded American Foundation for Equal Rights (afer.org) in 2009 and was very successful in raising the funds needed for this lawsuit.

So far, the Olson-Boies team has won. In the fall of 2012, the Supreme Court will decide whether to take this case as well as other important cases for LGBT rights such as the constitutionality of parts the Defense of Marriage Act.

This year, the Human Rights Campaign board made the bold move to appoint Chad as the president of the organization. We look forward to seeing his creative approaches and proven fund-raising skills put to work to accelerate reaching legal equality for LGBT Americans.

GOING WILD

A new organization, GetEqual—the brainchild of Paul Yandura and Jonathan Lewis—created quite a bit of good havoc by using civil disobedience techniques. Founded in 2010, they represent the spirit of the Dallas Principles: Full Equality Now. No Delays. No Excuses. Many politicians and their fundraisers state that they believe in full equality now. But they often mention that this is not the time. Of course, they believe in *equality now*, but in fact are working toward *equality later*. GetEqual, with their bold actions, is a key organization to raise awareness that we all need equality now.

GOING TO THE WHITE HOUSE

President Obama had promised to repeal Don't Ask, Don't Tell. Many actions helped to make it happen: the lawsuit won by Log Cabin Republicans, SLDN lobbying Congress, donors pushing key senators behind the scenes, a new organization, OutServe, of underground LGBT service members, and many other actions.

An action that was very different was Dan Choi and several others chaining themselves to the White House fence. It had a significant impact on the news and highlighted very publicly the need to repeal Don't Ask Don't Tell.

What should have been a small case of civil disobedience is becoming a bigger issue, as they got arrested and some of them are now awaiting trial.

GOING TO WORK

For thirty-eight years we have tried to have federal legislation to protect against employment discrimination. No results as of yet. So Tico Almeida, an employment attorney who worked as lead counsel in the U.S. House of Representatives on the proposal to ban workplace discrimination against LGBT Americans, decided to start Freedom to Work in the fall of 2011. This is a good example of focusing on a single Equality Goal to get the job done once and for all.

GOING TO CHURCH

There are multiple organizations that take the soft approach to work with different religious faiths to make them more accepting of homosexuality. Founded by Mitchell Gold in December 2005, FaithInAmerica.org takes a totally different approach by confronting directly the harm caused by religious bigotry. This is yet another example of a creative individual (he is the cofounder of Gold+Williams furniture design and manufacturing) acting differently. Mitchell Gold wrote an important book about LGBT, *Crisis: 40 Stories Revealing the Personal, Social, and Religious Pain and Trauma of Growing Up Gay in America*

GOING TO GRADUATE SCHOOL

Chuck Williams noticed an important gap in our tools to achieve LGBT legal equality: the need for rigorous, independent research and scholarship on issues of LGBT law and public policy. So he started the Williams Institute (WilliamsInstitute.law.ucla.edu) in 2001 and hosted it at the UCLA School of Law to demonstrate the seriousness and quality of the research. The Williams Institute has done pioneering research on the census and LGBT demographics, economic impact of marriage equality, parenting, safe schools, and much more.

GOING AFTER THEM

For many years, Mike Rogers reported, through his BlogActive.com website, about politicians that were in the closet while voting against equality. He helped change some of them to vote for equality.

In 2006, Mark Foley resigned from Congress after his explicit text messages and emails were publicized by Lane Hudson. This led to an outcry and many observers credit this case with helping the Democrats to gain back the House of Representatives.

In 2009, Kirby Dick released *Outrage*, a documentary about politicians who are in the closet and vote against equality.

GOING YOUR WAY

The stories above illustrate the importance of creativity and Acting Differently. Whether you are a volunteer, a donor, an activist, an ally, the head of an organization, or a bystander, by Acting Differently you can achieve what old methods have not.

The chapters that follow illustrate what motivated some people to take action. Read those chapters and find your own path—whichever fits your passion, your skills, and your means—and then do it. Dream on—and read on...

But even before starting, you may ask yourself—why bother? It is going to happen anyway!

49.

It Will Happen Anyway

Some people are saying: gays and lesbians (and to a certain extent, bisexual and transgender people) are now part of the popular culture. They have won (mostly) the culture wars. *So, why should I volunteer anymore or donate generously for achieving legal equality?* It is going to happen anyway!

Clearly, LGBT people are winning the hearts and minds of Americans as well as people around the world. But as this book points out, in the United States we are still far from being treated equally under federal and state law. eQualityGiving's Federal Equality Index stands at 15 percent. At the state level only two states (Connecticut and Vermont) provide full legal equality to its residents. Check all the details about the work to be done as presented in chapter 43.

This is not the time to give up the fight for three main reasons: first, there are plenty of periods in history in which there has been a backlash of acceptance of minorities. It can happen very quickly. Many times you just need a charismatic leader or a popular TV personality to move the country *backward*. For instance, if the country elects Mitt Romney, he has indicated that he would appoint to the Supreme Court very conservative judges in the mold of Scalia, Thomas, and Alito. Just this action, could set our legal equality back a generation or more.

Second, too many people are suffering and will continue to suffer until discriminatory laws are repealed and equality legislation is in place. They suffer in terms of the recognition and protection that their relationship deserves. They suffer because they cannot be legal parents. They suffer because they can be fired for being gay. They suffer bullying, and much more. They are not asking anything that will cost the government money (in fact, allowing same-gender couples to marry saves the government money and enhances the local economy). They are not asking for legislation that is difficult to create: update the laws that mention race, gender, national origin, religion by adding the words *sexual orientation and gender identity.*

Third, there is now a great momentum with volunteers, donors, organizations and most Americans supporting equality. We cannot stop now.

So, this is not the time to give up. We are really close.

Something very big occurred on May 9, 2012, that took us one step closer to equality: an acknowledgement by President Obama that when the founding fathers wrote

> We hold these truths to be self-evident, that all men
> are created equal

they actually meant it.

50.

What Happened on May 9, 2012?

This is the day that President Obama announced during a televised interview his support for the freedom to marry the person you love. It did not just "happen anyway." It happened because many people pushed for it. It was a momentous time. This was the first time that a sitting president of the United States of America indicated his support for full equality under the law for LGBT Americans. President Obama showed the leadership for *change* that enthralled so many people to vote for him in 2008. He showed the moral leadership that separate is not equal. Civil unions, which he used to support, are a separate and discriminatory institution (applying only to LGBT individuals).

When I went to the White House on May 4, 2009 at the invitation of President Obama, I gave him a letter that said in its entirety (with the italics and bold as in the original):

May 4, 2009

Dear President Obama,

Thank you for taking a moment to read this letter from a gay American.

I came to this country twenty-nine years ago with a Fulbright fellowship when America was the beacon of freedom. I got a doctorate from Stanford University, reached financial success, and retired at age forty. I became a citizen and lived the American dream.

But now America is no longer the leader in civil rights, as gay couples are not treated equally, like they are in many countries, including my former one, Spain.

Many American politicians are following your lead in a call for civil unions, a separate and unequal institution. You continue to express publicly your personal belief that marriage is between a man and a woman—which is clearly discriminatory and contrary to the practice of many religions, including your own.

When you say that you believe marriage is between a man and a woman, please know that those words feel like <u>a knife going through our hearts</u>. It is hurtful to us every time you say that, and it is harmful to our struggle for equal rights.

It would be helpful if you would instead say something like the following:

"As President, it is my duty to make sure all Americans are treated equally.

Our country is deeply divided on this issue.

*Some states allow same gender marriage, some civil unions and domestic partnerships, and some states forbid it in their state Constitutions. **The federal government needs to recognize and treat equally all marriage licenses issued by a state.***

*Marriage is also a religious institution. Since the US Constitution states that "Congress shall make no law respecting an establishment of religion, or prohibiting the free exercise thereof," **rest assured that the federal government will not interfere with religions' right to marry who they want. Some religions perform same-gender marriages, and other religions forbid it."***

I am available to discuss this matter with you or your aides at any time.

Sincerely, Juan Ahonen-Jover, Ph.D.

So when, three years and four days later, President Obama came out in favor of equal rights under the law for all Americans, this had two direct, personal implications for me.

First, most of Part IV of this book had to be rewritten. This book had a very different ending before May 9.

Second, my partner and I decided to do something more for our country. The next chapter discusses what we did.

51.

Why We Gave $10,000 to Obama

Visualize this for a moment: a gay couple in a white convertible with their fluffy white dog in the back. As they are driving down the Florida Keys, they learn the news that President Obama has publicly announced his support for same-gender marriage. So, right away they pull over to an Internet cafe to make a $10,000 donation to Obama's reelection campaign.

This is a true story, and, without the above fluffy details, was recounted on the front page of the *New York Times* on May 10, 2012.

I know it is true because my spouse and I are the couple in the story. So why did we do it?

This was not an emotional, impulsive decision because of Obama's support for the freedom to marry. We had thought about our position supporting (or not supporting) President Obama very carefully and for a very long time. But when Obama changed, so did we.

Before answering the question of why we did it, let me answer the reverse question.

WHY WE DID NOT GIVE TO OBAMA'S REELECTION CAMPAIGN BEFORE MAY NINTH

It is well known the importance of giving money early in a campaign. The sooner you give, the more the money can do. There was no doubt that President Obama would not have any significant opposition in a primary. So, why not give early?

Without any doubt, President Obama has done more for LGBT rights than all other presidents before him combined. While he has accomplished more, the bar was pretty low. Of the other previous forty-three US presidents, forty-one did nothing for

LGBT rights. One president (George W. Bush) pushed ruthlessly for constitutional amendments in the states discriminating against LGBT Americans for his political gain. Another president (Bill Clinton) appointed numerous LGB people (but not a single transgender person) to positions in his administration—but he twice signed devastating legislation discriminating against LGBT people ("Don't Ask, Don't Tell" and the "Defense of Marriage Act").

It was also clear to my spouse and I that we were voting to reelect President Obama. But we did not have the enthusiasm to work hard for Obama's reelection or give money to his campaign. We were not alone in this feeling. Yet our friends in the Democratic Party were begging us to be more enthusiastic, as if enthusiasm could be turned on or off at will. True enthusiasm comes from within. Like we felt when we voted for **CHANGE** (in all the campaign signs always in bold and in capital letters) in 2008. For us, our disappointment was clear-cut. It was not just because we disagreed with some of his most important policies or that he opposed the freedom to marry.

We did not give to him because he lacked moral leadership. The president was saying he supported all the benefits of marriage, but not marriage. He was saying that civil unions are OK. But civil unions are a separate and discriminatory institution. They are separate by statute, and they are discriminatory because they apply only to LGBT people. So he was telling the world that separate *is* equal. This was a profound lack of moral leadership, well beyond the marriage issue.

All of this changed on May 9, 2012. The president evolved and recognized finally that separate is not equal. He decided to personally support the fundamental right of people to marry the person they love. As we all know, allowing more people to marry does not devalue anybody's marriage, it only makes society more stable.

It is also clear that nobody is asking to change the freedom of any religion to marry whomever they want. But an essential component of the freedom of religion is to understand that some religions marry same-gender couples and others don't.

On the morning of May 9, 2012, before Obama made his announcement, I had given an interview to *Bloomberg News* addressing the issue of marriage equality. Then that very afternoon, the president made the announcement, and our world suddenly changed.

WHY WE GAVE $10,000 TO THE PRESIDENT'S REELECTION

For us it was not about what he had accomplished on LGBT issues. It is a good record, but we *expected* more. It is not about his major policies on other topics, many of which we disagree with. Neither was it because of his delivery on the promise of **CHANGE,** since, in our estimation, he has delivered SMALL CHANGE.

We donated because he took a very important moral stand. He loudly told the world what all Americans know: that separate is not equal. We needed our leader to take the morally correct stand that a majority of Americans believe: every couple should be able to express their love and commitment by being able to get married.

52.

Will President Obama Be Reelected?

Before we gave away $10,000, we considered, of course, whether President Obama could be reelected.

The question should actually be, how cannot he be reelected against a competitor who is not likable and has shown a propensity to support the one percent of the population (of which he is part) at the expense of the other 99 percent?

This should have been an easy reelection for President Obama. However, there are some important changes in the last four years in elections—powerful enough to change the outcome.

WHAT HAS CHANGED IN THE LAST FOUR YEARS

There are five changes that are new since 2008. Without them, it is quite likely that President Obama would be reelected with a comfortable margin, even after coming out in support of marriage equality. But with these changes now in place, the election could be very close.

1. *Counting the money: Big money in the election.*
   It is a completely new world, with the unlimited electioneering advertising that companies, unions, and individuals can do anonymously after the Supreme Court decision in 2010. This was a clear victory for conservatives and will play in their favor. Even Obama's fund-raising prowess will not be able to keep up.

2. *Voting: New voter registration regulations and voter IDs.*
   Several state legislatures controlled by Republicans have passed voter registration laws and voter ID requirements designed to disenfranchise groups like minorities, young voters who attend college, and elderly voters. All of these

groups tend to vote Democratic. This is another victory for conservatives.

3. *Counting the votes: Voting machines and faulty aggregation of results.*
   More than two hundred Democratic members of the House of Representatives cosponsored legislation to solve these problems. However, it was never put to a vote when the Democrats controlled Congress—a lost opportunity for the Democrats that could cost them this and future elections.

4. *CHANGE: Disappointment of the liberal base.*
   President Obama has chosen to support policies that are conservative (like Romney's healthcare plan in Massachusetts). And he has not done enough for combating climate change, or to close Guantanamo, or to protect legal rights for American citizens. *Politics is the art of expectations* and Obama has not done enough for those who were excited about his candidacy for **CHANGE**. Supporting marriage equality is an important step for those who want **CHANGE.** So is his new policy not to deport young people who are undocumented because they came to this country with their parents.

5. *We are the 99 percent.*
   Will the slogan and activities of Occupy Wall Street reappear this fall? I do not know, but they already made a significant contribution by highlighting that the vast majority of Americans are the 99 percent. In this presidential election, it is clear that Mitt Romney is not only part of the one percent, but also that he represents the interests of that one percent. Romney demonstrated this even more by selecting Representative Paul Ryan as his running mate. Representative Ryan has proposed to eliminate taxes on dividends and capital gains. This would mean a significant decrease in taxes for the very rich. For instance, on an income of more than 20 million dollars in 2010, Mitt Romney paid less than 15 percent of it in taxes (what was *your* tax rate?). If Paul Ryan's plan gets enacted, for the same income as in 2010, Mitt Romney would pay less than 1 percent in taxes. If voters really get to understand this, then Obama wins reelection—except if the super-rich pour one billion dollars in the election to have 50 percent of people vote against their own financial interests.

CAN OBAMA BE REELECTED BEING PRO–MARRIAGE EQUALITY?

Some Democratic political strategists are concerned about a potential barrage of political ads against Obama, in key conservative swing states, for being pro-marriage. They are concerned that this will cost him reelection.

First, consider that several influential Republicans leaders support marriage equality:

- Former Vice President Dick Cheney (whose daughter Mary got legally married in Washington DC to Heather Poe and have two children together).

- Former First Lady Laura Bush.

- David Koch, a billionaire who, with his brother Charles, has pledged to give a record $400 million to Republican candidates in the 2012 election cycle.

- Former Governor of New Mexico Gary Johnson, who is the 2012 nominee from the Libertarian Party for President of the United States.

- Former Secretary of State General Colin Powell.

- Ken Mehlman, former Chairman of the National Republican Committee as well as the campaign manager for George W. Bush's reelection campaign.

- Cindy McCain and Meghan McCain, wife and daughter of presidential candidate John McCain.

- Steve Schmidt, McCain's 2008 presidential campaign manager.

- David Blankenhorn, Founder and President, Institute for American Values, who wrote *The Future of Marriage,* a 2007 book *opposing* gay marriage.

Second, Republican attacks will be about everything. They attacked Obama for signing the healthcare act, which is a Republican plan. They attacked him for his policies that have improved the economy that had collapsed after eight years of Republican control. They even attacked him for getting Bin Laden. So, the fear of Republican attacks should not stop Obama from doing the right thing. He will be viciously attacked in any event, for any reason, real or imagined.

Third, a vote in a state against gay marriage cannot be reliably compared to a vote against Obama. A vote to ban same-gender marriage in a state is a separate question on a ballot. For instance, in 2008 Florida voted with a significant margin to forbid same-gender marriage in the state, but voters elected Obama there. Furthermore, now the vote would be against a sitting president, who has accomplished quite a bit (especially for moderate and conservative voters) and who is very likable personally (which is very important for reelections—just ask Presidents Reagan, Clinton, or G.W. Bush).

Fourth, voters want candidates who are strong leaders. A leader needs to show alignment between his internal beliefs and what he says. This alignment projects sincerity to the voters. It is an important part of trusting somebody. It also projects that he is a man (or woman) of conviction. Nobody on the right or the left believed that President Obama was evolving on marriage. The result was that people on the right and left were against him since they thought that he was a fake and believed in marriage equality anyway. People want strong leaders even if they disagree with them.

SO, CAN HE BE REELECTED?

The president has had many very solid accomplishments that should satisfy independents and moderate Democrats as well as moderate Republicans. Obviously, he is not going to get the vote of those who think, incorrectly, that he was not even born in this country or that he is a socialist. His main problem is going to be to motivate his base of supporters and those who voted for **CHANGE** in 2008. Most of the progressive voters, although unsatisfied, will come out and vote for him because they understand the alternative is worse. His biggest challenge will be motivating the youngest voters to go vote.

Although he has not delivered enough on promises that were important to young people (the environment, civil liberties, education, no tax cuts for the rich, etc.), coming out for the freedom to marry is meaningful to them—independently of whether they are gay or not. These young voters are in the age of dating and coupling, so marriage is on their minds. They have LGBT friends, and they understand that LGBT rights are the civil rights of our era. This is why Obama's support for marriage equality will be an important motivator for them to volunteer and to vote.

So, can he win reelection?

Yes, he can!

But only if he energizes his base that wanted **CHANGE,** and if he reminds people that most Americans are, by definition, the 99 percent, and if the economy remains stable (despite the economic problems in Europe and the refusal of Republicans to consider his job creation legislation).

The Republicans can help the reelection of President Obama if they continue attacking contraception, immigration, and Medicare.

But *will* he win reelection? Nobody knows, because it depends so much on the five key factors that have changed substantially the elections landscape in the last four years.

So, it is your turn—who do *you* support for president?

53.

Your Turn: Who to Support for President?

I have shown you my cards and told you why I support the reelection of President Obama. Now, it's your turn. If you are enthusiastic about reelecting the president, meaning that you will give to his campaign (according to your means) and/or volunteer your time, then you can skip this chapter. If not, please, read on.

In contrast to his predecessors from both parties, President Obama has achieved significant progress for LGBT rights:

- Signed into law the Matthew Shepard and James Byrd, Jr. Hate Crimes Prevention Act. This is important legislation that can assist states in prosecuting hate crimes. Note that it is not intended to be a replacement for state legislation also addressing hate crimes.

- Signed the repeal of Don't Ask, Don't Tell. Final negotiations to pass this bill crippled it. While it does allow service members to serve openly, it does not protect them against discrimination, like other minorities are protected. Furthermore, it does not recognize their spouse if they are legally married, resulting in unequal treatment of service members due to their sexual orientation. Furthermore, it does not address discrimination based on gender identity and expression.

- Changed more than thirty policies affecting the life of LGBT Americans.

- Declared that his administration would not defend the Defense of Marriage Act in court as it considered it unconstitutional. However, the administration will continue to abide by it until a court declares it unconstitutional or Congress repeals it. The Republican-controlled House of Representatives appointed a private attorney to defend

DOMA in court, paid by our taxes.

- Appointed more LGBT people to his administration that any other president at this point in the presidency.

- Was the first president to appoint transgender people to his administration. The three appointees so far are: Dylan Orr, Chloe Schwenke, and Amanda Simpson.

The most comprehensive, authoritative, and up-to-date list of the accomplishments of the Obama administration is here: eQualityGiving.org/Accomplishments-by-the-Administration-and-Congress-on-LGBT-Equality. It is written and updated by Andrew Tobias, a best-selling author, who is gay and is the treasurer of the Democratic National Committee.

But are these accomplishments enough?

Politics is the art of expectations. At the end of the day, it is up to each voter to decide whether the president and Congress have met their expectations. Obama could have done more on LGBT rights. In his direct control is signing an executive order requiring federal contractors to have nondiscriminatory employment policies. This executive order was approved by the Labor Department and the Department of Justice. But Obama's spokesperson has announced that he would not sign it this year.

Furthermore, realistically he could have pushed for a vote on ENDA in 2010. And the repeal of Don't Ask, Don't Tell should have included the clause, which was part of the proposed legislation, that LBGT people should not be discriminated in the military (service members can be open now, but they are not protected, as are other groups, against discrimination).

But even if many people had more expectations for **CHANGE,** Obama has done more than any president before him.

Mitt Romney, from an LGBT-rights perspective, is the opposite of Obama. While Obama is pro-equality, Romney is anti-equality:

- Romney opposes same-gender marriage.

- Romney is out of touch with the majority of Americans by opposing even civil unions.

- More damaging, he supports a Federal Marriage Amendment to the U.S. Constitution that would define marriage between one man and one woman only. What will happen to all the same-gender couples already legally married? Can you imagine if the government divorced you against your will? Or, if these marriages were preserved, what message are we sending to other people: some LGBT couples were allowed to marry while others won't?

- Romney opposes federal legislation protecting LGBT people from discrimination in employment, credit, housing, and public accommodations. This is a basic protection that most Americans assume that LGBT people have.

- Romney supports appointing conservative judges to the Supreme Court, in the mold of Justices Scalia, Thomas, and Alito.

Mitt Romney has solidified his anti-equality stance by selecting Representative Paul Ryan as his running mate. Ryan voted against the Hate Crimes Bill in 2009 and the repeal of Don't Ask Don't Tell in 2010. He also opposes not only marriage equality, but even civil unions.

In this day and age, it does not get much worse than this. Even the Log Cabin Republicans ran advertisements against Romney in 2008 while he was trying to get the nomination for the Republican Party. Although the Log Cabin, as a Republican organization, is prohibited from endorsing a Democrat, they could decide not to endorse anybody (they did not endorse Bush for reelection). So clearly, from an LGBT rights perspective, it would be very difficult for them to justify endorsing Romney. They might say that they support his other policies—smaller government, lower taxes, and so on. Or that they want to be insiders. All of these are weak arguments since they stand by the proposition that we are all created equal.

So, let's expand the discussion, for this chapter only, to other factors for supporting Obama, beyond that he is the first sitting president of the United States in favor of full legal equality for

LGBT people. Let's discuss how different groups of people may look at the next election.

If you are convinced that President Obama is a socialist, it might be good to look at the definition of socialism:

> A theory or system of social organization that advocates the vesting of the ownership and control of the means of production and distribution, of capital, land, etc., in the community as a whole.

Most dictionaries have basically the same definition; this one is from dictionary.com.

President Obama has done nothing that is even close to socialism. Even the "mandate" of buying private insurance is not socialism; it is de facto an expansion of the market for private insurance companies, which was proposed by Republicans in 1993 and implemented by Mitt Romney when he was governor. Obamacare is the same as Romneycare: both have the same individual mandate (or tax or penalty, as you may choose to call it).

Some people also think that President Obama is not eligible to be president since they do not believe that he was born in Hawaii or because he is not a natural born citizen (the "birthers" define natural born citizen as having a mother and a father both born in the US). Both arguments are particularly interesting now that Romney is the nominee for the Republican party:

- What else is there to say after the Hawaiian authorities have repeatedly confirmed that President Obama was born in Hawaii and that his birth certificate is authentic and made it public?

- Did you know that George Romney, father of Mitt Romney, ran for president in 1968 and that, beyond any doubt, he was not an American-born citizen? He ran for president illegally. Ask Mitt Romney where his father was born. Answer: his father was born in Mexico.

- If it was true (which isn't) that "natural born" in the US meant that both parents needed to be born in America, certainly President Obama would not be eligible for the presidency since his father was born in Kenya. Neither would be Mitt Romney, since his father was born in Mexico.

So beyond the people who think that President Obama is a socialist or not eligible for the presidency for not being a natural-born citizen (so Romney wouldn't be either), let's discuss other groups of people and how they may look at the presidency.

If you are an investor in the stock market the case for a Democratic president is very easy to make. Here is the analysis from Andrew Tobias, the best selling author of *The Only Investment Guide You Will Ever Need,* and treasurer of the Democratic National Committee:

> If you had invested $10,000 in the S&P in all 44 years since 1925 when Republicans held the White House, it would have grown—not counting dividends—to less than $30,000. But to more than $300,000 in the 44 years that Democrats (very much including Barack Obama) held the White House. So it could make self-interested financial sense to invest in our getting four more years.

If you are interested in job creation, President Clinton provided important data on September 5, 2012 during his speech at the Democratic convention:

> Since 1961, the Republicans have held the White House 28 years, the Democrats 24. In those 52 years, our economy produced 66 million private sector jobs. What's the jobs score? Republicans 24 million, Democrats 42 million!

If you are a *moderate* Republican, you should be happy with President Obama. Most of his policies are direct copy of moderate Republican policies (including healthcare and tax cuts). He has proposed historic budget cuts (four trillion dollars in cuts) that the Republican leadership of the House of Representatives (which is not moderate) has refused to consider. Under President Obama, *taxes are lower* than they were under both Bushes and Reagan. In national security, President Obama has proven to be a hawk. During his speech accepting the Nobel Peace Prize, he mentioned war thirty-two times and peace only seven times while justifying "just wars." He located and killed Osama bin Laden and several other terrorist leaders. And he has kept us safe from terrorist attacks.

For example, Andrew Sullivan, a well-known writer who is gay and self-identifies as a "conservative-minded independent," wrote a very eloquent support for President Obama's reelection on the Jan 16, 2012 issue of *The Daily Beast/Newsweek*.

Voters also need to consider the foreign bank accounts that Mitt Romney holds. Success is one thing. Having bank accounts in Bermuda, the Cayman Islands, and Switzerland and not disclosing details on them when you run for president of the United States is a big issue. And it does not pass the smell test.

Furthermore, running a business is very different from running a country. If *you* were ever to become unemployed, who would you like to be president? Obama, who has proposed job legislation multiple times and has extended unemployment benefits multiple times? Or Romney, with his Bain Capital experience of outsourcing and offshoring jobs, and cutting and slashing just to provide a better return to Bain and its investors?

As expected, and as intended, the policies of President Obama are clearly very attractive to independents as well as to moderate Republicans. So if you fall into one of these two Republican groups, your support to reelect Obama is very well justified.

The situation is different, however, for progressives who voted for **CHANGE.** The president has delivered only SMALL CHANGE, whether in terms of offshore drilling, climate change, human rights for detainees (including American citizens), separation of church and state, faith-based initiatives, wars, closing Guantanamo, stopping "too big to fail" banks, or negotiating the extension of the Bush tax cuts to the wealthiest. In all of these critical issues, his policies have been conservative, and, over time, they will show to be a detriment to the country as much as it was when President Clinton supported the repeal of the Glass-Steagall Act, requested by Republicans, which was a significant factor in the 2008 financial crisis.

The concern is that many young people who became enthusiastic about the candidacy of then Senator Obama have become disillusioned because of the SMALL CHANGE.

President Obama did bring **CHANGE,** fortunately, when he supported the right of people to marry the person they love. So, if you are an LGBT person, this **ONE HUGE CHANGE** justifies all by itself your enthusiastic support for his reelection. This means giving money for his campaign (even in modest amounts) and volunteering for it if you have the time. But the *most important* thing that you can do is talk to your friends, coworkers, family members, Facebook friends, and e-mail and text everybody about the importance of this election and going to vote (they should check before election day that they are properly registered!). Turnout will be critical to the president's reelection.

But if you are a progressive and not gay and disappointed with SMALL CHANGE, what do you do then? If you live in a non-battleground state, vote your conscience and even vote for a third-party progressive candidate (if any is running in your state). In battleground states, as much as it is upsetting, if you are a liberal you need to be sure to vote for President Obama, for the alternative is clearly worse. Under a Republican administration the culture wars will be emboldened, not only against LGBT people, but also about the use of contraception, freedom of choice, and more.

Ultimately, the big differentiator between the two candidates is who they are going to appoint to the Supreme Court. Given that four of the nine justices are over seventy years old, one could expect one or more vacancies during the next four years. President Obama has a record of appointing two very qualified and fair-minded candidates to the Supreme Court. One can expect that this track record will continue, especially understanding how well he knows potential candidates, given his experience as a constitutional professor.

On the Republican side, candidate Romney has appointed Robert Bork as cochair of his Justice Advisory Committee. Bork is a right-wing extremist who was voted down to be a Supreme Court justice by the biggest margin in US history. So, Romney could have not indicated more clearly his support for an ultraconservative Supreme Court. To be more explicit, Romney has also stated that he would appoint conservative people who are similar to Alito, Scalia, and Thomas to the Supreme Court *and the federal bench.*

So, if you are a progressive upset about getting only SMALL CHANGE, the reality is that you need to go to vote and support the reelection of President Obama, because his opponent would bring big change to the Supreme Court that could affect our country not for just four years, but for our lifetimes.

Some readers may think that this chapter is overtly partisan. Actually, it was completely rewritten after President Obama came out for marriage equality. The version with Obama not supporting marriage equality had a very different ending. The difference between Obama and Romney could not be starker now. If you want to help Obama's reelection, a very good electronic tool is their Dashboard (my.barackobama.com/page/content/dashboard-signup).

While liberals may need to compromise while voting to reelect President Obama, this is not the case when supporting candidates for other offices across the nation, as the next chapter discusses.

54.

Your Turn: Supporting Other Candidates

You can support candidates in four main ways:

- by voting for them
- by giving them money
- by volunteering for them (fundraisers, phone banking, etc.)
- by motivating your friends to do the same

If you have the means and/or time, you can accelerate achieving legal equality by helping elect pro-equality legislators to Congress and state legislatures. You are not constrained by supporting just your local candidates, who might not be so good on equality. There are plenty of candidates across the country who support full LGBT equality. This means that an LGBT person or ally can focus on only these candidates for financial support and volunteering.

But even savvy donors and volunteers fall, from time to time, into the trap of supporting candidates with more rhetoric than track record working for our issues. There is really little to no justification nowadays for an LGBT person supporting *any* candidate who is not *fully* pro-equality (i.e., supports *all* the Equality Goals, including marriage).

You may hear this argument: support this candidate so that he or she can learn more about our issues. Frankly, just point the candidate to this one-page questionnaire: www.eQualityGiving.org/Endorsement-Form. If they cannot answer yes to all the questions, politely tell them that they can learn about all the Equality Goals at eQualityGiving.org (or hand them a copy of this book). No need for you to spend your money or energy teaching them. There are plenty of other candidates who support equality enthusiastically and should receive our also enthusiastic support.

Actually, there are so many pro-equality candidates (see the list for federal and statewide races at www.eQualityGiving.org/Endorsed-Candidates) that a donor could reach the federal limits just donating to them (a donor could also donate unlimited funds using a super PAC).

THREE THINGS YOU CAN DO FOR PRO-EQUALITY CANDIDATES

When you donate to or volunteer for candidates, remember to do three things:

1. *Help them:* give money, fundraise for them, volunteer, or do a house party, etc.

2. *Tell them*: you are an LGBT person who expects them to support legislation to bring legal equality.

3. *Follow up:* after the election, congratulate them and follow up to see if they pass legislation to bring legal equality.

The importance of these three steps were highlighted by donor Charles Merrill, a bisexual, who is coauthor of The Dallas Principles and heir to the Merrill-Lynch fortune:

> Too often, LGBT money and support is welcome during an election, and at its conclusion, the issues that are most important to the community are placed on the back burner.

IF YOU CAN SUPPORT SEVERAL CANDIDATES

If you are able to help several candidates (with money or volunteering), then the rest of this chapter is for you. If in the past you have given only to nonprofits, consider giving also to political candidates and political organizations. These donations are not tax-deductible, but elected officials are a strategic component for reaching legal equality. Consider giving to as many of these groups as your resources permit:

- Give to the *presidential race*. The Supreme Court is divided five to four, and several judges could retire soon.

- Give to *candidates in your state* who have been endorsed by eQualityGiving. Personal contact is critical:
  - Attend one or more fundraisers for them (or better yet, organize one).
  - Meet them personally and thank them for supporting equality.
  - Come out to them as lesbian, gay, bisexual or transgender.
  - Explain to them that you support pro-equality legislation. *Follow up* after the election to remind them about *passing legislation*. But never ask for a promise to pass legislation because you gave them money or supported them in any other way. This is illegal.

- Give to politicians who you *know personally* if they are in a competitive race. Personal relationships are critical. If they are not in a competitive race, explain why you are giving to others.

- Give to the eQualityGiving-endorsed candidates in states other than your own.

- Give to *state candidates* recommended by Gill Action, HRC, and other political organizations.

- Give to *LGBT candidates* endorsed by the Victory Fund.

- Give to *political organizations:*
  - National Stonewall Democrats, if you are a Democrat
  - Log Cabin Republicans, if you are a Republican
  - LGBT Council of the Democratic National Committee. Note that in this case the money is branded as LGBT (which is important), but the funds are used for general campaign expenses. The Republican National Committee does not have an equivalent fund.

In conclusion, support only candidates who are fully pro-equality.

Voting is a different issue, since you may not have a choice in your particular district to vote for a fully pro-equality candidate. The next chapter discusses this and other issues regarding voting.

55.

Your Turn: Voting

A friend—a woman from Florida, who is an independent and always votes for "the person"—said yesterday, "This year I am voting Democratic down the line. I am tired of gridlock." This friend represents well how many Americans think about politics:

- Vote for the person, not the party

- Vote for different parties in the White House, Senate, and House to have checks and balances

Both stances are correct—to a certain extent. It is certainly important to vote for somebody who is personable, like George W. Bush or Barack Obama—both liked by many people. But at the end of the day, it is their ideas and policies that make the difference. This is why some people dislike George W. Bush—because of his ideas and policies. Similarly, this is why some people dislike Barack Obama.

In the current election, Obama is more likable than Romney, but it still is important to vote for the ideas they represent. One represents the 99 percent; the other one is part of, and clearly represents, the interests of the 1 percent.

The second stance, about checks and balances, is worthwhile, of course. The issue is that it has been abused so extensively that has brought intransigence and gridlock. In the Senate, Republicans have used the filibuster (to basically require sixty votes to pass anything) so much more compared to any time in our history. This is not a democracy as explained in the Robert's Rules of Order (Webster's New World, page 244) which quotes Henry Robert in 1876:

> Where there is radical difference of opinion in an organization, one side must yield. The Great lesson for democracies to learn is for the majority to give the minority a full, free opportunity to present their

side of the case, and then for the minority, having failed to win a majority, gracefully to submit and to recognize the action as that of the entire organization, and cheerfully to assist in carrying it out, until they can secure its repeal.

The Senate minority leader, Republican Mitch McConnell repeatedly stated immediately after the 2008 election that their number one goal was to ensure that President Obama would be a one-term president. This is very different from the more appropriate goal of putting country first and working to pass legislation to solve the country's problems.

In the House, controlled by the Republicans, the votes have become so uncompromising as derailing negotiations of raising the debt ceiling in the summer of 2011, to the point that the nation's credit was downgraded for the first time in our history. This is not good for our country.

But this election is not about whether President Obama did a good job getting us out of the second largest recession in our history (of course, recovery from such a huge recession is slow). This election is about choosing among two different visions for our future: strengthening our commitment to the basic social services of Medicare, Social Security, and Medicaid or dismantling them.

Mitt Romney clearly indicated his preference by choosing Representative Paul Ryan as his running mate. Paul Ryan has advocated tirelessly to convert Medicare into a voucher system, privatize Social Security, and limit the payments to the states for Medicaid.

So, like the wise friend in Florida, this time it is worth voting Democrat down the line. It's about not only avoiding gridlock and getting things done, but about preserving the type of caring society that we developed since the New Deal.

Or, as Congressman Barney Frank summarized in a bumper sticker he had printed: "Vote Democratic: We're not perfect, but they're nuts."

Let's now move on to another important topic related to voting.

56.

Your Turn: Ballot Initiatives

As we have discussed in chapter 42, human rights of a minority should not be put to a majority vote. Do you expect that a majority would give equal rights to a minority?

This is why in the United States we have three branches of government. As much as we do not expect a majority to vote for the rights of a minority, it is often difficult for lawmakers (elected by a majority) to pass legislation for the rights of the minority. This is why we have the judiciary branch, which should be independent of interference by the legislature and popular vote.

As expected, the thirty-two states that put on the ballot measures limiting marriage to between one man and one woman were all successful (except for Arizona, where the measure was defeated once and then passed two years later). These ballot initiatives were used to draw conservatives to the polls. Karl Rove and Ken Mehlman, Bush campaign manager, used this technique extensively. Mehlman, who is gay, has since apologized for turning against his own community.

In November 2012, we face ballot initiatives in four states: Maine, Washington, Maryland, and Minnesota.

Maine was the first state in the nation to pass a marriage equality bill by the legislature; the governor signed it on May 6, 2009. Immediately after, the opposition was successful in stopping it from going into effect by winning a referendum by popular vote, 53 to 47 percent in November 2009. Now the supporters of marriage equality are putting the following initiative in the November 2012 ballot:

> Do you favor a law allowing marriage licenses for same-sex couples that protects religious freedom by ensuring no religion or clergy be required to perform such a marriage in violation of their religious beliefs?

Polls in June 2012 show 57 percent support for it, so there is a good chance to win it. This campaign is organized by Mainers United for Marriage: www.MainersUnited.org.

Washington state legislators approved marriage equality early this year, and it was signed into law by Governor Christine Gregoire. However, enough signatures were gathered to put the law to a popular vote on November 6, 2012. A June 2012 poll shows support for the law at 51 percent, against 42 percent opposing it and 7 percent undecided. There is a good chance to win this vote. Besides polling well so far, large companies in the state such as Microsoft, Boeing, Starbucks, and Amazon are all supportive. A coalition of organizations is working to win marriage equality under the name of Washington United for Marriage: www.washingtonunitedformarriage.org.

Maryland faces a ballot initiative to stop the Civil Marriage Protection Act from taking effect. This law confers marriage equality and was approved by the legislature and signed by Governor O'Malley. This anti-equality initiative was placed on the ballot by the conservative and religious right. Until recently, there were substantial questions about the chances of defeating such a ballot initiative. First, this campaign will be very expensive, given the cost of the media markets in Maryland, especially during a presidential election year (which also requires placingg many advertisements to be noticed). Second, the polls indicated a slight preference from the voters to defeat the ballot initiative. But in polls asking for equal rights, one needs to count between 3 and 6 percent of the responders who indicate their support for equality in a poll, but will vote the contrary in the secrecy of the ballot box.

President Obama's coming out for marriage equality brought an immediate increase in support for marriage equality in Maryland, including now, for the first time, from a majority of African-Americans in Maryland. A May 2012 poll puts the support for marriage equality at 57 percent of all voters.

So this will be an expensive battle, but it can be won. The campaign site is: www.MarylandersForMarriageEquality.org.

Note that losing the ballot initiative in Maine, Washington, or Maryland does not place a constitutional amendment forbidding marriage among two same gender individuals.

However, *Minnesota* faces a constitutional amendment that will define marriage as between a man and a woman. In May 2012 it was polling even. This battle is winnable, given enough resources. Minnesotans United for All Families is managing this campaign: www.mnunited.org.

In the next chapter, let's discuss how you can help reach legal equality.

57.

How Much Is Equality Worth to *You?*

Equality just doesn't happen on its own. Many people give substantial amounts of money, time, and talent to make it happen.

The culture of giving is important, independently of how much money you have. Consider any of the ideas below (or create your own) depending on your financial situation:

1. *Give a few dollars*
   Most people can donate ten, twenty, or fifty dollars from time to time. Even a five-dollar gift helps. No matter how much you can afford, giving helps bring equality.

2. *Give a percentage of your annual income*
   This is a common formula. For example: give 10 percent of your annual income, as some religious traditions suggest— tithing toward a worthy cause.

3. *Give a percentage of your net assets (or your assets in stock investments)*
   Some experts believe that if you spend less than four percent per year of your invested assets, you will not run out of money in your lifetime, while your assets will still keep up with inflation. Of course, this is based on many assumptions, so you need to check with your financial advisor.

4. *Give a percentage of your disposable income*
   Deduct from your income your basic expenses: mortgage, income taxes, and basic living expenses. Then give a small part of what's left to advance equality.

5. *Give a part of your annual bonus*
   In their minds, people do not count bonuses as part of regular income. So why not use part of it to obtain your legal rights (for example, to ensure that you or a loved one cannot

be fired solely for being a lesbian, gay, bisexual or transgender individual)?

A SIMPLE GIVING PLAN

There are many causes that deserve your money, but if you or someone you love is lesbian, gay, bisexual, transgender why not give first to promote fundamental fairness?

It is easy to create a giving plan. Start by considering three main buckets in which to put your money:

1. Amount you want to give in the next twelve months to advance LGBT equality: $_____

2. Amount you want to give in the next twelve months to other LGBT issues: $_____

3. Amount you want to give in the next twelve months to non-LGBT issues: $_____

For the amount that you want to give to advance equality (first bucket) consider the following split:

- 40 percent for politicians and political organizations that will assist in passing legislation for equality. In election years, maybe this should be 60 percent;

- 40 percent for nonprofits working to achieve equality. In election years, maybe this should be 30 percent;

- 10 percent for opportunity giving. In election years, maybe this is reduced to 5 percent; and

- 10 percent for social-obligations giving. In election years, maybe reduce to 5 percent.

These percentages are just a guideline. Modify them to suit your interests, but it is important to stick to an allocation that makes sense for you and your interests.

Of course, if you do not have the means at this time, still consider giving a little—just a few dollars. A culture of giving will do wonders for your spirit.

If you have the means, the next chapter is for you—otherwise, just skip it.

58.

Strategic and Creative Donors

Advances in equality have occurred because of the dedication and sacrifices of many grassroots volunteers, elected officials, and staff people working for nonprofits, and many people fortunate enough (and generous enough) to fund the movement.

This chapter focuses on big donors, and discusses fourteen different strategies they can follow for their giving.

There are many terms used to describe strategic philanthropy: intelligent giving, strategic giving, effective philanthropy, venture philanthropy, inspired philanthropy—donors, especially mega donors, can create a unique combination of strategies that best fit their needs—for more details on these strategies, including online resources, please check www.eQualityGiving.org/Giving-Center.

1. IMPACT GIVING

Donors concentrate their giving on a few organizations, political candidates, or Equality Goals with *large* donations that have a significant impact.

Good for:

- donors with a large budget, and
- donors with a solid strategic vision that can change the movement.

2. GOAL GIVING

Donors concentrate their giving on achieving a goal instead of concentrating on an organization.

Good for:

- donors passionate to achieve a specific goal (e.g., safe schools or marriage equality), and
- donors who are very strategic and have access to detailed information about the goals.

3. ORGANIZATIONAL GIVING

Donors concentrate most of their giving on a single organization.

Good for:

- members of the board of that organization as well as its senior employees, and
- donors whose professional interests match the organization direction (e.g., an attorney giving to a legal defense organization).

4. CONCENTRATED GIVING

Donors give to a limited number of organizations and political candidates.

Good for:

- donors with a more limited budget, and
- donors focused on a specific Equality Goal.

5. DISPERSED GIVING

In this strategy, donors give to a multitude of organizations and political candidates.

Good for:

- donors with a large budget;
- donors who have a hard time saying no; and

- donors who fundraise for another cause—this approach creates goodwill among donors who support each other's causes.

6. OPPORTUNITY GIVING

Donors give to take advantage of an immediate opportunity that will achieve a tangible result in a short period of time (usually a year or less).

Good for:

- donors who want to see immediate results.

7. CAPACITY GIVING

Donors give to build the capacity of an organization or political party and make them more robust over a long time.

Good for:

- donors who know and trust the senior leadership of the organization and believe in the potential of its mission.

8. LOCAL GIVING

Donors give to organizations and politicians in their local community and state.

Good for:

- donors who want to make a tangible difference in the life of their community, and
- donors who want to get to know and influence their local and state politicians.

9. MAVERICK GIVING

Donors who want to give to unconventional causes or lesser-known organizations/politicians.

Good for:

- donors who like to create new paths.

10. ANGEL GIVING

Donors who give to help new organizations get established.

Good for:

- donors interested in social entrepreneurship.

11. GAP GIVING

Donors review each of the Equality Goals and each of the strategic approaches to achieve LGBT equality and give to the areas that are insufficiently funded.

Good for:

- donors with considerable financial means, and
- donors interested in strategic analysis.

12. COLLABORATIVE GIVING

Donors give jointly with other donors in the pursuit of a common goal. Examples of this approach are giving circles and some foundations. There are two flavors to collaborative giving: (1) donors give to a fund and a committee distributes the money; or (2) donors are presented with a set of options, and they decide individually how much to give to each of the options.

Good for:

- donors sharing a common passion, and

- donors who do not have the time to or interest in analyzing the different options available.

13. CONVEYOR GIVING

Donors decide on a goal to be achieved and search for the proper organizations or groups to help achieve it jointly. Donors in effect convey together a group of organizations for a joint goal.

Good for:

- donors with significant giving capability,
- donors respected by the groups that they are conveying, and
- donors with the time and ability to bring together different groups.

14. SOCIAL GIVING

Donors give based on social obligations and requests from friends.

Good for:

- donors who do not want to say no.

If you are a big donor, you can use one or more of the strategies presented to maximize the impact of your giving, taking into account your personal situation.

The next chapter will show how to apply these donor strategy ideas to supporting LGBT organizations.

59.

Your Turn: Supporting Organizations

This chapter is for people who are (or want to become) donors to organizations for equality. Before you think about supporting an organization, think about what Equality Goal you are most passionate about. Is it marriage? Is it employment nondiscrimination? Is it freedom of gender? Or another one? Then reread the chapter of this book in Part II that discusses that goal. You will see mentioned there good organizations whose mission is aligned with that goal. Of course, there are other good organizations (especially at the state level) that may not be mentioned in this book.

Another approach is to focus on the paths to reach equality instead of a specific Equality Goal. These paths are discussed in Part III of this book. Focusing on a path is very appropriate if you have a specialty that matches it. For instance, if you are an attorney, your focus may not be on a single goal, but to reach equality through the courts.

Or if your focus is religion, check organizations focused on this such as the InterfaithAlliance.org, and the ReligiousInstitute.org. For a different perspective on religion, check FaithInAmerica.org.

When giving to nonprofit organizations, consider these tips:

- *Give for multiple years.*
  Some people recommend three-year commitments, but your commitment should be until a specific goal is reached.

- *Give consistently.*
  In election years, it is very tempting to give more for political issues at the expense of the nonprofits. Organizations need stability, so continue supporting them despite that this might be the "election of a lifetime."

- *Check outcomes.*
  What has the organization achieved each year for equality? How relevant is this to achieving legal equality? Is the organization actually doing what they said they were going to do?

- *Help with unplanned opportunities.*
  In a perfect world, organizations would know what they are going to do for the whole year. In reality, events change and require funding to take advantage of a new development. For example, an organization may need extra money to fund a survey on a new development. This is not an excuse for organizations that do not plan properly. It is helpful to be there for well-managed organizations that want to make the best of a new situation.

For the next chapter, let's turn our attention to specific actions you can take to support equality.

60.

Your Turn: Twenty Actions *You* Can Take *Now*

You want more ideas of what to do? Here are twenty actions for you, compiled out of eQualityThinking, the first free, open, and virtual conference for full LGBT equality. Over a period of ten weeks, with a team of eleven volunteer organizers, we produced sixteen hours of panels with eighty-two prominent panelists and twenty-seven question moderators. It was refreshing to hear the thought processes of some of the brightest and most experienced minds working for LGBT equality as well as the passion and commitment of our youth. All the calls were recorded and you can hear them at: www.eQualityThinking.org. Now it is time to put these ideas into action. Choose, among the proposed actions, those that are more appropriate for you.

1. **HELP REELECT PRESIDENT OBAMA AND A DEMOCRATIC CONGRESS**
   With just a few weeks to go, nothing is more important than reelecting President Obama because he is the first pro-equality sitting president. Mitt Romney is exactly his opposite by being against same-gender marriage, even against civil unions, and against federal nondiscrimination protections.

   Similarly, we need Democrats to control both houses in Congress—otherwise equality legislation won't be brought for a vote.

   Your action is to enthusiastically convince your family, friends, coworkers, acquaintances, and neighbors to first check that their voting registration is still valid, and then vote on November 6, 2012. And, if you have the capability, donate and volunteer.

2. MAKE POSSIBLE THE APPOINTMENT OF FAIR JUDGES

It is critical for our equality to elect a president who can appoint fair judges to the Supreme Court and federal courts. Our investment in the legal organizations and legal actions cannot produce the best results without fair judges. Obama and Romney are exact opposites about the type of judges they will appoint to the Supreme Court and to the federal bench. In effect, by appointing fair judges, Obama can accelerate LGBT integration in society as full citizens, or Romney can delay it by a generation or more by appointing anti-equality judges.

3. HELP GETTING EQUALITY THROUGH THE COURTS NOW

While the election is going on, our legal organizations are winning very important cases on equality. Litigation is one of the most cost-effective ways of gaining equality, so your continued support of the legal organizations is very important at this time. This is one of the most effective tools at our disposal. Listen to what our top LGBT legal organizations are battling and assist them: www.eQualityGiving.org/eQualityThinking-Getting-Equality-Through-the-Courts.

4. DO MAKE IT BETTER FOR OUR YOUTH

After the heart wrenching campaign "It Gets Better" by Dan Savage, the issue is how we can *make it better* for our youth *now*. This is a topic that you need to bring up at every town hall meeting for Republicans and Democrats alike. Ask Governor Romney and running mate Paul Ryan why they did not tape a "It Gets Better" video like the president and vice president did (as well as the secretary of state, and many Democratic leaders).

Check the discussion with two Democratic members of Congress on how to make it better: www.eQualityGiving.org/eQualityThinking-We-Will-Make-It-Better. Also, listen to our youth talking about their issues and activism—very impressive: www.eQualityGiving.org/eQualityThinking-Your-Passion-Your-Voice.

5. **CHANGE THE DIALOG ABOUT RELIGION'S ROLE**
Because of President Obama's full support for marriage equality, you can expect backlash from some religious people. Reread Part I of this book to be prepared for the debates that will ensue with family, coworkers, and friends. Also, listen to this panel of leaders from different religions. One of the eye-opening highlights of the discussion was that they do not want politicians *to use religion as an excuse for their legislative actions*: www.eQualityGiving.org/ eQualityThinking-God-and-Gays.

6. **BUILD BRIDGES WITH CORPORATE AMERICA**
One of the new challenges after the Citizen's United decision is that a corporation may give a grant to your favorite LGBT organization while at the same time secretly donate to elect legislators who do not support our equality under the law. One of the significant gaps in our movement, and in the progressive movement in general, is that we do not have a database of corporate giving to politicians and candidates. This is not easy to do without legislation requiring disclosure of donors, but it is critical.

Listen to the thoughtful discussion about building bridges with corporate America: www.eQualityGiving.org/ eQualityThinking-Building-Bridges-with-Corporate-America.

7. **SUPPORT NEW MEDIA AND SOCIAL MEDIA**
This is an important component of winning in 2012. It is a flashy place to invest. But check the financials of each group, since some of them are operating out of a shoestring, while others have raised quite a bit of money (and continue asking for more). For more information, listen to a panel about these organizations: www.eQualityGiving.org/ eQualityThinking-New-Media-Social-Media-Pathways-for-LGBT-Equality.

8. **GET MORE STATES WITH MARRIAGE EQUALITY**
There are three states facing a ballot initiative this November to allow LGBT people to marry: Maine, Maryland, and Washington. Minnesota is voting on a

constitutional amendment this November not to allow marriage or civil unions. If you live in one of these states, it is very important that you help since you will be affected directly. If you are a supporter of the freedom to marry, help independently of where you live.

9. **HELP WITH STATE ISSUES**

Do you know where your state stands on equality under the law? Take this thirty-second test: www.eQualityGiving.org/ Equal-and-Gay-Quiz.

The good news is that we are fully equal under the law in two states (Vermont and Connecticut). The bad news is that we are unequal in 96 percent of the states. Check here where your state stands and help now: www.eQualityGiving.org/ States-of-Equality-and-Gay-Rights-Scorecard.

10. **ASK FOR FULL EQUALITY**

We will never get full equality if we do not ask for it. Review the Equality & Religious Freedom Act (Omnibus Equality Bill) written by Karen Doering, Esq., and introduced by eQualityGiving on March 18, 2009 (www.eQualityGiving.org/Blueprint-for-LGBT-Equality).

We need legislation that is comprehensive and does not negotiate away our equal rights even before it is introduced. Ask Congressman Polis (www.FearlessCampaign.org) to introduce such legislation instead of a compendium of existing bills.

11. **HELP PASS FEDERAL EQUALITY LEGISLATION**

Listen to US Senator Merkley and Congresswoman Baldwin discuss—during a one hour session—how to pass LGBT legislation in the Senate and the House: www.eQualityGiving.org/eQualityThinking-Opportunities- for-LGBT-Equality-in-this-Congress.

And then help push, push, and push, because all fair-minded members of Congress should embrace equality.

12. HELP PASS FULL NONDISCRIMINATION FEDERAL LEGISLATION

Most Americans assume that we are already protected against discrimination. We are not. It is difficult to be out and fight for other things if you are not secure in your employment and other basic civil rights.

According to Barney Frank, the main sponsor of ENDA, it is going to be difficult to pass ENDA in 2012. As you are supporting pro-equality candidates for Congress, explain to them the advantages of truly comprehensive nondiscrimination legislation, such as the American Equality Bill, based on expanding the Civil Rights Act to include sexual orientation and gender identity: www.eQualityGiving.org/American-Equality-Bill.

13. ACTING DIFFERENTLY

New organizations and many individuals are taking direct action. This is something important to support along with the conventional approaches to reach LGBT equality. Listen to these people who are acting differently, including with civil disobedience, and support them and join them if you can: www.eQualityGiving.org/eQualityThinking-Acting-Differently-Civil-Disobedience-Direct-Action.

14. ENSURE GOVERNANCE WITH FULL L+G+B+T REPRESENTATION

The board of directors that govern the LGBT organizations needs to fully represent the movement. Work with the boards and executive directors of the organizations that you are involved with to ensure full representation. There is particular need of more transgender board members. Eighteen of our largest national LGBT organizations do not have a single transgender board member. Check this Transgender Board Member Resource: www.eQualityGiving.org/Transgender-Board-Members.

Also, you can listen to this prominent panel about the perils of tokenism: www.eQualityGiving.org/eQualityThinking-The-T-in-LGBTQ.

15.**SUPPORT THE SCIENCE AND PRACTICE OF CHANGING HEARTS AND MINDS**
Media campaigns are very expensive, so it is a very good investment to support those who are studying the science and practice of how to change hearts and minds. Check the work of these researchers involved in it:
www.eQualityGiving.org/eQualityThinking-Changing-Hearts-and-Minds.

16. **IF YOU ARE A DONOR, TAKE MORE RISKS**
We all get comfortable with a certain level and way of giving. We all need to stretch more and be more generous. Maybe think of giving using new approaches to reach equality. Listen to this very frank and enlightening discussion with four well-known donors, and consider additional approaches to your giving: www.eQualityGiving.org/eQualityThinking-How-Can-Donors-Accelerate-Equality.

Also listen to three of our next-generation donors: www.eQualityGiving.org/eQualityThinking-Your-Passion-Your-Voice.

17. **DO SOMETHING ABOUT HIV CRIMINALIZATION**
Some of the most insidious laws against anyone with HIV refer to criminalizing HIV. And the extent of these laws is not known even by very well-informed people.

Listen to examples of these laws in our land and internationally: www.eQualityGiving.org/eQualityThinking-Why-HIV-Criminalization-Matters.

18. **SUPPORT EQUALITY THROUGH MOVIES**
Movies can reach wide audiences and help inform as well as change hearts and minds. Hear about these projects before anybody else, directly from five filmmakers, producers, and writers: www.eQualityGiving.org/eQualityThinking-Your-Passion-Your-Voice.

19. **THINK REALLY BIG AND DIFFERENTLY**
What if we could have an organization of the size and

effectiveness of the NRA or AARP lobbying for our rights? This is the idea behind the National Parents Association. Learn about it: www.eQualityGiving.org/eQualityThinking-Final-Panel.

20. **LAST, BUT NOT LEAST: DON'T ACCEPT ANY MORE EXCUSES**
There is always a good excuse for delaying equal rights. But as Dr. Martin Luther King, Jr. said, *"A right delayed is a right denied."* Read The Dallas Principles in appendix 2.

Follow up with the status of pro-equality legislation in: www.ActOnPrinciples.org.

61.

Your Turn, Your Way

So many Equality Goals, so many paths to reach equality, so many priorities: how do you choose?

Choose your goal based on your *passion*.

Choose your path based on your *skills*.

If you have the passion, the skills, and the proper resources for the task (money or time) you can push for equality your own way— without following the established paths.

For example, Dan Savage created, basically single-handedly, the important campaign "It Gets Better." Within two months, President Obama and many others in his administration had produced a video to tell LGBT youth that it gets better.

One more example: a donor friend saw a need in his town to help LGBT high school seniors to have their own prom so they could be themselves. He made it happen for $1,500. It has been among the most satisfying giving in his (generous) career as a philanthropist.

Final example: another friend has studied the new restrictive registration laws in Florida. He has determined ways to comply with them at a minimum cost so that the maximum number of people can be registered. His efforts may make the difference between winning and losing this critical battleground state.

So, how do you go about going your own way?

Consider these four approaches:

1. *The Highway*
   In this approach you basically go through an established organization (maybe you are on its board, or are a volunteer or donor).

Here are the steps that you follow:
1. Have an idea
2. Discuss the idea
3. Present the idea to board
4. Improve the idea based on feedback
5. Get approval for the idea
6. Fundraise to pay for it
7. Do it!

2. *The Shortcut*
   Here you just do it yourself. No bureaucracies.
   1. Have an idea
   2. Do it!

This works very well if you are a very creative person and just use standard (and free) tools such as Facebook, Twitter, YouTube, blogs, and others.

3. *The Expert's Way*
   In this case you become an expert (for example, in election law) and help make a big step forward for equality. This method requires talent and much patience, since it is very time-consuming. But it is priceless.

4. *No Road*
   In the ultimate freedom, you decide not to follow any of the paths above. Just do some constant random acts that move us closer to equality. Be creative. The dots will connect one day.

If you can go your own path and are very creative, you can have a very significant impact. Remember Apple's commercial quoted at the beginning of Part IV of this book:

> Here's to the crazy ones, the misfits, the rebels, the troublemakers, the round pegs in the square holes... because the people who are crazy enough to think that they can change the world are the ones that do.

Is this you? It certainly is *me*. The next chapter presents my own path.

62.

My Turn, My Way

This book is not about theories about equality or reporting about what others have done. It is all based on things that I have done myself.

The path I chose for equality was very simple. First, identify what is the goal (I created the term *Equality Goals*). Second, determine the steps required to achieve those goals. Third, create the tools to make this a reality.

In summary, gaining equality under the law is all about creating the intellectual framework of what needs to be done and then creating the tools to do it. In reality, I am a tool creator. These tools help others to accelerate reaching equality. I ended up working with many people who use the tools and make it happen.

So here is what this is all about in more detail:

1. **IMMEDIATE GOAL: EQUAL UNDER THE LAW**
   Other goals, such as social justice or equality in real terms, are longer term. But the most necessary goal is to reach equality under the law.

   TOOL CREATED: Equality Goals
   By comparing the protections of what other groups have and the LGBT people do not have, it is easy to set the Equality Goals—the protections under the law that we are missing. These goals were explained in detail in Part II of this book.

   TOOL CREATED: eQualityGiving.org website
   This website is focused on how donors can accelerate achieving LGBT legal equality. It is organized based on the Equality Goals. All other major LGBT organizations arrange their websites by issues (which are very different from goals).

2. EQUALITY GOALS IN LEGAL TERMS

Once you have the Equality Goals, it is important to write them in legal terms so that they can be enacted as legislation.

TOOLS CREATED: Omnibus Equality Bill and American Equality Bill
These tools serve to tell legislators: this is what we want—no more, no less than other groups. Basically, this *is* the Gay Agenda.

These proposed bills also serve as model bills, so that, even if legislation is introduced affecting only one part that is covered in the Omnibus bill, it serves as a reference in case that the bill gets watered down before passage. This legislation was written at my request by Karen M. Doering, Esq.—a great lawyer specializing in nondiscrimination law.

The American Equality Bill, championed by J. Todd Fernandez, Esq., is the subset of the Omnibus Bill that focuses on adding the terms *sexual orientation* and *gender identity* to the Civil Rights Act.

3. STRATEGY TO REACH THE EQUALITY GOALS

Once we have identified the Equality Goals, it is easy to determine the basic strategy. Which goals are better addressed in states, and which ones at the federal level? What's the priority? What's the investment required?

TOOL CREATED: Strategic Matrices
These matrices address the questions above in a clear manner. They are available at www.eQualityGiving.org/Giving-to-Charity-Guide.

TOOL CREATED: Discussion Network
A network of major and mega donors, executive directors of LGBT organizations, pro-equality elected officials and endorsed candidates, and thought leaders who discuss how to achieve LGBT equality.

4. CANDIDATE ENDORSEMENT

Since the main objective is to be equal under the law,

candidate endorsements are very important—since candidates are the future legislators who will vote for our equality.

TOOLS CREATED: Endorsement Framework and Endorsed Candidates list
The framework is unique. Nothing similar is publicly available: www.eQualityGiving.org/Endorsements.

This framework is used for actual endorsements, in which every candidate submits a questionnaire which can be made public and is personally interviewed (with the exception of President Obama, with whom I spoke but not in a formal endorsement interview): www.eQualityGiving.org/Endorsed-Candidates.

My spouse, Dr. Ken Ahonen-Jover, interviews all the candidates and coordinates the endorsement process.

5. **FOLLOW THROUGH**
   After the elections, it is very important to follow through and ensure that legislation is being introduced, voted on, and passed.

   Is a bill ready to be voted on? How many votes do we have? To answer these questions, the leadership of the House and Senate conduct whip counts, in which they poll members of their own party about their position on a piece of legislation. Whip counts are also conducted at the state level. Lobbyists conduct their own whip counts (although usually partially, since it is very labor-intensive).

   TOOL CREATED: ActOnPrinciples.org
   This is a unique tool that makes whip counts public and allows a registered user to update the whip count. There is nothing like it anywhere else. The tool is kept up-to-date by Donald Hitchcock.

   TOOL CREATED: Platform for Other Contributors
   By creating a versatile platform, specific web pages can be created very quickly that allow others to manage important projects. For example:

1. Andrew Tobias, Treasurer of the Democratic National Committee, created and keeps updated the most comprehensive list available of accomplishments by the Administration and Congress on LGBT equality: www.eQualityGiving.org/Accomplishments-by-the-Administration-and-Congress-on-LGBT-Equality

2. Ret. Captain Tom Carpenter, Esq., created the list of issues pending after the repeal of Don't Ask, Don't Tell: www.eQualityGiving.org/DADT

3. Dr. Dana Beyer leads the project to have more transgender board members so that the governance of our organizations represent the full spectrum of L+G+B +T: www.eQualityGiving.org/Transgender-Board-Members

6. **MEASURE PROGRESS**
Once you have clear goals, it is imperative to measure progress.

TOOL CREATED: Federal LGBT Legal Equality Index
It is available here: www.eQualityGiving.org/Equal-Protection-of-the-Law

TOOL CREATED: States of Equality Scorecard
This includes an evaluation of every state based on the Equality Goals; it can be sorted by state, by score, and by goal. It is available here: www.eQualityGiving.org/States-of-Equality-and-Gay-Rights-Scorecard

In addition, you can take the quick quiz to guess the score of your state (or any state): www.eQualityGiving.org/Equal-and-Gay-Quiz

7. **URGENCY—THINK BIGGER—ACT DIFFERENTLY**
We need a constant sense of urgency to achieve the Equality Goals, because too many people are suffering, legal equality is needed right now. To do so, the movement needs to think bigger and act differently.

TOOL CREATED: THE DALLAS PRINCIPLES
I convened the meeting of twenty-four leaders that created The Dallas Principles, which are described in detail in chapter 31 and appendix 2 of this book and also available online: www.TheDallasPrinciples.org

TOOL CREATED: eQualityThinking
This was a unique conference, described here: www.eQualityThinking.org and in chapter 60.

The final tool is this book; it includes all my prior work, but it goes well beyond it and is addressed to a wide audience: not only LGBT people and their allies, but to *all persons* who—independently of their religion or political affiliation—believe in the equality expressed in the United States Declaration of Independence and in the Constitution.

63.

Summary: All Out

Imagine yourself writing the 2013 edition of *The Gay Agenda* (if there was ever to be one). What will it say?

That mostly depends on what happens on Tuesday, November 6, 2012. If President Obama gets reelected and the Democrats have a majority on both chambers in Congress, we can expect an accelerated path to treat all citizens equally under the law.

If Republicans win the presidency or control either chamber of Congress, we can expect almost a complete halt of progress for legal equality—all of that despite any good efforts that our friends at Log Cabin Republicans will make, and despite any efforts from a handful of Republican legislators that otherwise would have voted for equality.

If Republicans control any of the houses, *they will not bring any pro-equality legislation for a vote.* If Mitt Romney becomes president, you can be sure that he will nominate for the Supreme Court ultraconservative judges—as he has repeatedly pledged. We cannot expect these judges to rule for equality.

So even if you agree with Republican principles, do you want to *delay for a generation* your equality and the equality of your friends? If you say that you are not a single-issue voter, then go ahead and vote for lower taxes for the super rich and fewer services for everybody else (which is basically a single issue). If you prefer lower taxes and smaller government to your being treated as a first-class citizen, I respect your choice, but there is nothing else I can say.

For everybody who prioritizes dignity over money, here is what you can do between now and November 6, 2012:

1. If you are an independent, a moderate Republican, or a blue-dog Democrat: clearly President Obama is your man. His policies clearly fit your philosophy, so go out and do all you

can, every day, for his reelection. They do not come better than him. You should also vote Democrat down the line, to stop the gridlock.

2. If you are a liberal: Obama is *not* your man. You will not get liberal policies out of him. But, at least he is the first sitting president to come out in favor of legal equality for all citizens, and this is **ONE HUGE CHANGE**. Equality is a bedrock principle on which all Americans should agree (we should, but in practice we don't). So pinch your nose, tell all of your friends to get out and vote for President Obama and Democrats down the line. If you live in a safe Democratic district and state, then you can vote for candidates in liberal parties.

3. If you are a conservative: on fiscal matters, Obama has lowered the taxes more than any of the Bushes or Reagan. Do you realistically think that the taxes can get any lower under Romney without jeopardizing basic services like Medicare? On military issues, Obama has killed Osama bin Laden. Do you realistically think that Romney, who has no military and no foreign experience, will be stronger than Obama?

4. If you are pro-equality and independently of your political philosophy: you should fund the work of LGBT legal organizations. There are several cases that are very close to being presented to the Supreme Court and can be won in the current Supreme Court—so they need now the resources to succeed.

Choose your own path to help. You may have lots of time and no cash—then volunteer. You may have cash and no time—then give. Do whatever fits your means, time, personality, passion, and skills. The more that you can think bigger and act differently, the better. What is at stake is whether we can reach legal equality now, or if will it take another generation. What is at stake is whether *each of us*, independently of our race, our gender, our religion, our national origin, our sexual orientation, our gender identity and expression, and our disability will be protected against discrimination in our jobs, will be able to marry the person we love, will be able to be ourselves, will be able to form a family, and will have our children safe in school.

In summary, will our country live up to the promise in our constitution, will our country live up to our bedrock principle that every person should be treated equally under the law?

This is what is at stake on November 6, 2012.

A Respectful Message for *You*

- **To President Obama:** *Thank You for Your Leadership on Equality.*

- **To Governor Romney:** *Please Respect our Constitution.*
  How can you support a constitutional amendment to our beautiful constitution to add discrimination in marriage? How can you *not* support the principle of equality under the law?

- **To legislators:** *Equality Under the Law Is What Makes the United States of America a Great Country.*
  Every day that you delay enacting equality legislation, you are affecting real people, and you are not complying with your oath of office.

- **To a religious person:** *Protect Your Freedom of Religion.*
  Your freedom of religion is only possible if others have freedom of religion. This means that we cannot write civil laws based on any particular religion.

- **To parents and grandparents:** *Your Family's Values.*
  You determine what your family's values are. Do you love your children equally? Do you treat them equally? Do you want others to do the same?

- **To teenagers:** *Bullying Is Not Cool.*
  Bullies are immature, cruel, and insecure. Definitely, not cool.

- **To LGBT teenagers:** *We Will Make It Better.*
  Teenage years are always difficult—more difficult because of the immature bullies. But truly, it gets better. And a bunch of us are working every day to make it better now.

- **To bullies:** *We Know Your Game.*
  You might be an immature and cruel teenage bully, not understanding the harmful effects that bullying has on somebody's life. Or you might be an adult political bully,

intentionally misleading people about what family values are, or what freedom of religion entails, or what the constitution really means, and in doing so harming the lives of many people.

But we Americans now know your game and will stand up to protect our constitution, our family values, our individualism, our freedom of religion, and our inherent right to happiness—*game over.*

Epilogue: The Ultimate Goal

The gay agenda is simply to fulfill the American promise that every person is treated equally under the law—independently of their sexual orientation (heterosexual, homosexual, or bisexual) or their gender identity or expression. So it affects every single person.

Imagine living in a country in which:

- each of us is respected and has an opportunity to develop to our maximum capacity;

- each of us can pursue happiness on our own terms;

- a religion's laws—whether from Bahai, Buddhism, Christianity, Hinduism, Islam, Judaism, Mormonism, or others—are not imposed on non-members;

- the courts are truly independent;

- each of us is judged by our actions and not judged because of the color of our skin, our gender, our race, our national origin, our disability, our religion, our sexual orientation, or our gender identity or expression.

This country already exists and it is bound by a great constitution. Let us all work to ensure what we all believe in: equal treatment under the law.

What needs to be done is known. Time is of the essence because the current unequal treatment causes real damage to real people. So, let's work for

Full legal equality now. No delays. No excuses.

As you know from reading this book, full equality under the law is the next step, but what is the ultimate goal?

The ultimate goal is a world without prejudice.

As Mother Theresa said: "If you judge people, you have no time to love them."

The fact is that achieving a world without prejudice is a very difficult goal to reach. But it can be reached, because each of us has the power to stop prejudging others right now.

May we all become inspired and live without prejudice.

Thank *You!*

Countless people engaged daily in achieving equality for the LGBT community have influenced the thoughts expressed in this book and in the eQualityGiving website (where parts of this book appeared first).

These people include the twenty-three other authors of The Dallas Principles; all the members of the Discussion Network of eQualityGiving; the eighty-two panelists and twenty-seven question moderators of eQualityThinking; the webmaster, editors, and champions of Act On Principles; the elected officials eQualityGiving has endorsed over the years; the speakers and participants at OutGiving; and the executive directors and staff of equality organizations who work so hard to achieve equality.

Thanks to my editor Jennifer Lynn and to the kind people who endured reading a draft of this manuscript. Special thanks to those who provided many detailed comments that improved this book. They are: Dr. Dana Beyer, David Cockrell, Stephen Herbits, Michael Krawitz, Janice Langbehn, Dr. Sailesh Rao, and Paul Yandura.

But more than anybody else, my appreciation and love is for Dr. Ken Ahonen-Jover. He is my soul mate, best friend, sounding board, and spouse.

About the Author

Juan Ahonen-Jover, Ph.D, is an entrepreneur who did well and is now doing good. He is the creator and cofounder of eQualityGiving, ActOnPrinciples, and eQualityThinking, all focused on the fundamental principle that everyone should be treated equally under the law.

Juan was awarded a Fulbright Fellowship and was educated at Stanford University in supercomputers and business. He has four advanced degrees and is fluent in four languages. He co-authored a book on computers and is an innovator in election protection.

Juan enjoys speaking engagements from time to time. Contact him at www.GayAgenda2012.com.

APPENDIX 1:

Notable LGBT People

This appendix lists a few lesbian, gay, bisexual, and transgender people (LGBT) who are particularly notable. The list is not comprehensive, by any means. We cannot understand the Gay Agenda without knowing some of the LGBT figures and their contributions to society.

How do we know that these people are gay, lesbian, bisexual, or transgender? Some cases are easy, since the person publicly announced his or her sexual orientation or gender identity. For others there is plenty of historical evidence, while still others are more disputed. If you want to learn more about their contributions to society or their coming out status, Wikipedia has good write-ups about them.

POLITICS AND GOVERNMENT

- **Johanna Sigurdardottir** (1942–). Lesbian. Current Prime Minister of Iceland since 2009.

- **Elio di Rupo** (1951–). Gay. Current Prime Minister of Belgium since 2011.

- **Per-Kristina Foss** (1950–). Gay. For a brief period in 2002, served as Prime Minister of Norway.

- **Bertrand Delanoe** (1950–). Gay. Current Mayor of Paris since 2001.

- **Klaus Wowereit** (1953–). Gay. Current Mayor of Berlin since 2001.

- **Annise Parker** (1956–). Lesbian. Current Mayor of Houston since 2010.

- **Christine Quinn** (1966–). Lesbian. Speaker of New York City Council.

- **Barney Frank** (1940–). Gay. Member of the US House of Representatives (1981–2013). Chairman, House Financial Services Committee (2007–2011). First member of Congress to marry a same-gender spouse (2012).

- **Tammy Baldwin** (1962–). Lesbian. First female elected from Wisconsin to the US Congress and first openly LGBT person elected to the US Congress (1999–).

- **Jared Polis** (1975–). Gay. Member of the US House of Representatives (2009–).

- **David Cicilline** (1961–). Gay. Member of the US House of Representatives (2011–).

- **Gerry Studds** (1937–2011). Gay. First Member of Congress to come out while in office.

- **Harvey Milk** (1930–1978). Gay. Member of San Francisco Board of Supervisors, who was murdered along with Mayor Moscone by a fellow supervisor.

- **Nancy Wechsler** (1950–). Lesbian. First open LGBT person elected to office in the United States (Ann Arbor City Council, 1972).

- **Waheed Alli** (1964–). Gay. Muslim. Member of the House of Lords, British Parliament.

- **James McGreevey** (1957–). Gay. Governor of New Jersey (2002–2004).

- **James Hormel** (1933–). Gay. Philanthropist. First openly LGBT ambassador to the United States (Luxembourg, 1999). Appointed during recess (Senate wouldn't confirm him).

- **Michael Guest** (1957–). Gay. U.S. Ambassador to Romania (2001–2004). First openly gay ambassador to be confirmed by Senate. Retired in 2007 in protest for LGBT discrimination in the State Department.

- **J. Edgar Hoover** (1895–1972). Presumed gay. First director of the FBI (1935–1972).

- **Eleanor Roosevelt** (1882–1962). Presumed lesbian. First Lady of the United States (1933–1945).

- **Barbara Jordan** (1936–1996). Lesbian. Member of the US House of Representatives (1973–1979). Leader of the Civil Rights movement.

- **Deborah Batts** (1947–). Lesbian. First openly LGBT person to be appointed as federal judge (1994 by President Clinton).

- **Georgina Beyer** (1957–). Transgender. World's first open transgender individual to be elected to Parliament (New Zealand, 1999).

- **Edward II** (1284–1327). Presumed bisexual. King of England.

- **Frederick the Great** (1712–1786). Presumed gay. King of Prussia (1772–1786).

- **Ferdinand I of Bulgaria** (1861–1948). Bisexual. Tsar of Bulgaria. Declared Bulgaria's independence from the Ottoman Empire.

RELIGION

- **Rev. Troy Perry** (1940–). Gay. Founder, Metropolitan Community Church.

- **Archbishop Carl Bean** (1944–). Gay. Founder, Unity Fellowship Church Movement. Made famous the song "I Was Born This Way" in 1977, well before Lady Gaga.

- **Gene Robinson** (1947–). Gay. Episcopalian Bishop of New Hampshire—first of any major Christian religion.

- **Bishop Mary Douglas Glasspool** (1954–). Lesbian. First open lesbian to become bishop in the Anglican faith.

- **Rabbi Sharon Kleinbaum** (1959–). Lesbian. Senior Rabbi of the largest LGBT synagogue in the world.

- **Rabbi Stephen Greenberg** (1956–). Gay. First openly gay Orthodox rabbi.

- **Imam Daayiee Adfullah** (1954–). Gay. American Muslim imam. Co-director, Muslims for Progressive Values. Board member, Al-Fatiha Foundation.

- **Irshad Manji** (1968–). Lesbian. Canadian Muslim author, journalist, and advocate. Director of Moral Courage Project and NY University. Books: *Allah, Liberty and Love*; *The Trouble with Islam Today*. Documentary: *Faith Without Fear*

- **John McNeill** (1925–). Gay. Theologian and former Jesuit. Author of multiple books, notably *The Church and the Homosexual* (1976).

- **Rev. Malcolm Boyd** (1923–). Gay. Priest, author of more than thirty books, and civil rights activist. Came out as gay in 1977.

- **Mel White** (1940–). Gay. Clergyman and writer: *Stranger at the Gate; Lust: The Other Side of Love*.

MILITARY

- **Alexander the Great** (356–323 BC). Presumed gay. Emperor, who by age thirty had expanded his domain from Greece to Persia and to Egypt. One of the most successful military commanders of all time.

- **Hadrian** (76–138 AD). Presumed gay. Fourteenth Emperor of the Roman Empire.

- **T. E. Lawrence, "Lawrence of Arabia"** (1888–1935). Presumed gay. Liaison during the Arab Revolt. Writer: *Seven Pillars of Wisdom*.

- **Tammy S. Smith** (1963–). Lesbian. Brigadier General, U.S. Army. First openly LGBT general in the United States military.

SCIENCE

- **Alan Turing** (1912–1954). Gay. Father of computer science and artificial intelligence. Mathematical genius who broke German codes during WWII. His breakthroughs shortened WWII and saved thousands of lives.

- **Baron John Maynard Keynes** (1883–1946). Bisexual. One of the most influential economists ever.

- **Lynn Conway** (1938–). Transgender. Creator of the methodology used to design all computer chips. Also invented method for high-performance computers.

- **Sally Ride** (1951–2012). Lesbian. Astronaut, physicist, engineer, and educator. First American woman in space. Youngest American to go into space (age 32).

- **Joan Roughgarden** (1946–). Transgender. Professor emeritus of biology, Stanford University. Author of eight scientific books.

- **Ben Barres**. Transgender. Chair, Neurobiology, Stanford University School of Medicine.

- **Deirdre McCloskey** (1942–). Transgender. Professor of economics, University of Illinois at Chicago. Author of numerous books.

SPORTS

- **Martina Navratilova** (1956–). Lesbian. Tennis player. All-time career record for men or women in singles and doubles.

- **Greg Louganis** (1960–). Gay. Four Olympic gold medals and five gold World Championships for diving. Best-selling author: *Breaking the Silence*.

- **Mildred "Babe" Zaharias** (1911–1956). Lesbian. One of the greatest athletes of the twentieth century. Two gold and one silver medals in 1932 Olympics. Multitalented: golf, basketball, track and field.

- **Toller Cranston** (1949–). Gay. Figure skater. Canadian national champion. Bronze in 1976 Olympics.

- **Renee Richards** (1934–). Transgender. Ophthalmologist, tennis player, and author.

- **Billie Jean King** (1943–). Lesbian. Professional tennis player.

- **Johnny Weir-Voronov** (1984–). Gay. American figure skater. Three time US national champion.

- **Billy Bean** (1964–). Gay. Former Major League baseball player and author. Came out in 1999. Book: *Going the Other Way*.

- **Glenn Burke** (1952–1995). Gay. Former Major League baseball player. First and only Major League player known to be out to his team while a player.

- **Ian Roberts** (1965–). Gay. First rugby player to come out (1995).

BUSINESS

- **Sir Cecil Rhodes** (1853–1902). Presumed gay. Mining magnate. Founder of African state of Rhodesia. Funder of Rhodes scholarships.

- **Tim Cook** (1960–). Gay. CEO of Apple (2011–). One of the highest-paid executives ever ($376 million stock award in 2011).

- **Chris Hughes** (1983–). Gay. Cofounder, Facebook. Owner and publisher, *The New Republic*.

- **Peter Thiel** (1967–). Gay. Venture capitalist. Early investor in Facebook.

- **Tim Gill** (1953–). Gay. Cofounder of software company Quark. Philanthropist and activist: Gill Foundation and Gill Action, which together invest about $20 million a year to promote equality for LGBT people.

- **David Bohnett** (1956–). Gay. Cofounder of GeoCities, sold to Yahoo in 1999. His foundation has given more than $45 million in grants.

- **Jon Stryker** (1958–). Gay. Billionaire heir to Stryker corporation. Philanthropist.

- **Jonathan Lewis** (1958–). Gay. Progressive Insurance. Investor and visionary philanthropist.

- **Linda Ketner** (1950–). Lesbian. Heiress to Food Lion fortune. Business consultant and philanthropist.

- **Bruce Bastian** (1948–). Gay. Cofounder, WordPerfect. Philanthropist.

- **Martine Rothblatt** (1954–). Transgender. Attorney, author, and entrepreneur. Founder and CEO, United Therapeutics.

- **Kathy Levinson** (1956–). Lesbian. Former chief operating officer and president, E*Trade. Three-sport varsity athlete. Philanthropist.

- **Megan Smith** (1965–). Lesbian. Senior executive, Google.

- **Mitchell Gold**. Gay. Cofounder, Mitchell Gold+Bob Williams furniture. Cofounder, Faith In America. Philanthropist.

- **Bob Page** (1945–). Gay. Founder, Replacements Limited. Philanthropist.

- **Charles Merrill, Jr.** (1920–). Bisexual. Author, artist, and philanthropist. Son of Merrill-Lynch founder.

- **Michael Bishop** (1942–). Gay. Businessman. Majority owner of BMI airline, which he sold to Lufthansa. Net worth around $800 million.

LITERATURE AND THEATER

- **William Shakespeare** (1564–1616). Presumed bisexual. Poet and playwright. Considered greatest writer in the English language.

- **Tennessee Williams** (1911–1983). Gay. Writer and playwright: *A Streetcar Named Desire, Cat on a Hot Tin Roof*, and more.

- **Hans Christian Anderson** (1805–1875). Presumed gay. Most famous writer of fairy tales.

- **Walt Whitman** (1819–1892). Gay. Father of free verse. One of the greatest American poets.

- **Virginia Woolf** (1882–1941). Lesbian. Writer: *Mrs. Dalloway, To the Lighthouse, Orlando, A Room of One's Own*, and more.

- **Truman Capote** (1924–1984). Gay. Writer: *Breakfast at Tiffany's, In Cold Blood*, and more.

- **Gore Vidal** (1925–2012). Gay. Writer: *The City and the Pillar, The Best Man, The Last Empire*, and more.

- **André Gide** (1869–1951). Gay. Writer. Nobel Prize for Literature, 1947.

- **Ralph Waldo Emerson** (1803–1882). Bisexual. Writer. Leader of the Transcendentalist movement based on self-reliance.

- **E. M. Foster** (1879–1970). Gay. Novelist: *Where Angels Fear to Tread, The Longest Journey, A Room with a View, A Passage to India, Maurice*, and more.

- **Oscar Wilde** (1854–1900). Gay. Playwright and novelist: *The Importance of Being Earnest; Salome, The Picture of*

Dorian Gray,

- **Thomas Mann** (1875–1955). Bisexual. Nobel Prize for Literature, 1929. Works: *Buddenbrooks, The Magic Mountain, Death in Venice,* and more.

- **James Baldwin** (1924–1987). Gay. Writer and civil rights activist. Books: *The Fire Next Time, Go Tell it on the Mountain,* and more.

- **Simone de Beauvoir** (1908–1986). Bisexual. Influential philosopher and writer. Companion of philosopher and author Jean-Paul Sartre.

- **Gertrude Stein** (1874–1946) and **Alice B. Toklas** (1877–1967). Lesbian couple. Writers, art collectors.

- **Dustin Lance Black** (1974–). Gay. Screenwriter. Oscar winner for *Milk* (Best Original Screenplay, 2008).

- **Sir Terence Rattigan** (1911–1977). Gay. Famous British playwright.

- **Harvey Fierstein** (1952–). Gay. Actor and playwright: *Torch Song Trilogy, La Cage aux Folles, A Catered Affair.*

- **Jean Cocteau** (1889–1963). Gay. French writer, artist, and filmmaker. Member: American Academy, French Academy, Royal Academy of Belgium, and German Academy.

- **Federico García Lorca** (1898–1936). Gay. Poet, dramatist, and theater director. One of the most important poets in the Spanish language.

- **Paul Verlaine** (1844–1896). Gay. Renowned French poet.

- **Arthur Rimbaud** (1854–1891). Gay. Prodigy French poet. Had long-term relationship with Paul Verlaine.

- **Armistead Maupin** (1944–). Gay. Writer: *Tales of the City.*

- **Alan Ball** (1955–). Gay. Writer, director, actor, producer. *American Beauty* (Oscar for Best Original Screenplay), *Six*

Feet Under.

- **Andrew Tobias** (1947–). Gay. Writer about investments, coming out, other topics. Innovator in insurance. Treasurer, Democratic National Committee.

- **Reinaldo Arenas** (1943–1990). Gay. Best-selling writer of *Before Night Falls, Farewell to the Sea.*

- **W. H. Auden** (1907–1973). Gay. Famous poet.

MUSIC

- **Pyotr Ilyich Tchaikovsky** (1840–1893). Gay. Russian composer of classical music.

- **Leonard Bernstein** (1918–1990). Gay. Renowned American composer and conductor.

- **Sir Elton John** (1947–). Gay. Singer, songwriter, and composer.

- **"Boy George"—George Alan O'Dowd** (1961–). Gay. Singer and songwriter.

- **George Michael** (1963–). Gay. Musician, singer and songwriter.

- **Cole Porter** (1891–1964). Gay. Composer and songwriter. Married Linda Lee Thomas. His parties in Paris were renowned.

- **Joan Baez** (1941–). Bisexual. Folksinger and songwriter.
- **Ricky Martin** (1971–). Gay. Singer and actor.

- **Whitney Houston** (1963–2012). Presumed bisexual. Singer. Actress. The most-awarded female act of all time.

PAINTING, SCULPTURE

- **Leonardo da Vinci** (1452–1519). Presumed gay. Painter, sculptor, architect, scientist, musician, and inventor. One of the greatest geniuses of all time.

- **Michelangelo** (1475–1564). Presumed gay. One of the most famous painters, sculptors, architects, poets, and engineers of the Renaissance.

- **Andy Warhol** (1928–1987). Gay. Artist. Leader of the Pop Art movement.

- **David Hockney** (1937–). Gay. Pop art painter, printmaker, and photographer.

FASHION

- **Cristobal Balenciaga** (1895–1972). Gay. Fashion designer. Founder of the Balenciaga *haute couture* house.

- **Gianni Versace** (1946–1997). Gay. Fashion designer. Founder of the Versace label.

- **Charles Nolan** (1957–2011). Gay. Fashion designer. Founder of the Nolan label.

- **Tom Ford** (1961–). Gay. Fashion designer. Founder of the Ford label. Movie Director: *A Single Man.*

MOVIES, ENTERTAINMENT, TV

- **Rock Hudson** (1925–1985). Gay. Actor who died of AIDS. His movies include: *Magnificent Obsession, Giant, Ice Station Zebra,* and *Dynasty.*

- **Sir Ian McKellen** (1939–). Gay. Actor.

- **George Takei** (1937–). Gay. Actor: *Star Trek.*

- **Angelina Jolie** (1975–). Bisexual. Actress, director, and humanitarian.

- **Rosie O'Donnell** (1962–). Lesbian. TV show host, actress, comedian.

- **Ellen Degeneres** (1958–). Lesbian. Comedian, actress, TV show host.

- **Anderson Cooper** (1967–). Gay. Reporter, author, and TV anchor.

- **Rachel Maddow** (1973–). Lesbian. Author and TV host.

- **Don Lemon** (1966–). Gay. TV host.

- **Alvin Ailey Jr.** (1931–1989). Gay. Founder, Alvin Ailey American Dance Theater in New York.

- **Josephine Baker** (1906–1975). Bisexual. Singer, dancer, actress, and activist. Significant contributions to the Civil Rights movement.

- **Rudolph Valentino** (1895–1926). Presumed gay. Famous actor in silent movies. Known as the Latin Lover. Married twice to women who presumably had lesbian relationships.

- **Marlon Brando** (1924–2004). Presumed bisexual. Actor. Named by the American Film Institute as the fourth greatest male American actor of all times. The book *Brando Unzipped* claims he had relationships with other famous actors, including James Dean, Cary Grant, John Gielgud, and Montgomery Clift.

- **Cary Grant** (1904–1986). Bisexual. Actor. The American Film Institute named him the Greatest Male Star of All Time. Movies: *The Philadelphia Story; To Catch a Thief; An Affair to Remember; North by Northwest...*

- **Sir John Gielgud** (1904–2000). Gay. Actor, director, producer. One of few to win an Oscar, a Tony, an Emmy, and a Grammy.

- **Montgomery Clift** (1920–1966). Bisexual. Actor: *From Here to Eternity, A Place in the Sun, Confess,* and more. Nominated four times for Academy Awards.

- **Greta Garbo** (1905–1990). Bisexual. Actress: *Anna Christie, Grand Hotel.*

- **James Dean** (1931–1955). Gay. Iconic actor: *Rebel Without a Cause, East of Eden,* and *Giant.*

- **Anthony Perkins** (1932–1992). Gay. Oscar-winning actor. Died of AIDS.

- **Sir Laurence Olivier** (1907–1989). Presumed bisexual. Renowned actor and director.

- **Tab Hunter** (1931–). Gay. Actor: *Battle Cry, That Kind of Woman.*

- **Suze Orman** (1951–). Lesbian. Financial advisor, author, TV host.

- **David Geffen** (1943–). Gay. Film, theater, and music producer: *ET* and *Saving Private Ryan.*

- **Chaz Bono** (1969–). Transgender. Writer and musician. Child of entertainers Sonny and Cher.

- **Ismail Merchant** (1936–2005) and **James Ivory** (1928–). Gay couple. Founders, Merchant Ivory productions. Films: *A Room with a View, Maurice, Mr. and Mrs. Bridge, Howards End.*

- **Pier Paolo Pasolini** (1922–1975). Gay. Film director and writer. Films: *Teorema, Canterbury Tales.*

- **Luchino Visconti** (1906–1976). Gay. Film, opera, and theater director. Films include *Death in Venice, The Leopard,* and *The Dammed.*

- **Pedro Almodóvar** (1949–). Gay. Oscar-winning Spanish filmmaker: *All About My Mother. Talk to Her.*

CIVIC ENGAGEMENT

- **Harry Hay** (1912–2002). Gay. Renowned LGBT rights activist. Cofounder: Mattachine Society, Radical Faeries.

- **Del Martin** (1921–2008) and **Phyllis Lyon** (1924–). Lesbian couple. Renowned feminists and gay-rights activists. Founders of Daughters of Bilitis.

- **Frank Kameny** (1925–2011). Gay. Astronomer. Activist. Created slogan *"Gay is Good."*

- **Bayard Rustin** (1912–1987). Gay. Civil rights leader. Main organizer of the 1983 March on Washington.

- **Jane Addams** (1860–1935). Lesbian. First American woman to win the Nobel Peace Prize (1931).

- **Leonard Matlovich** (1943–1988). Gay. Vietnam War veteran, Purple Heart and Bronze Star. Tombstone reads: "A Gay Vietnam Veteran—When I was in the military, they gave me a medal for killing two men and a discharge for loving one."

- **Roberta Achtenberg** (1950–). Lesbian. First openly LGBT person, whose appointment required US Senate confirmation (1993, asst. secretary of Housing and Urban Development). Currently, commissioner, US Commission on Civil Rights.

- **Chai Feldblum** (1959–). Lesbian. Professor of law, Georgetown University. Chair, Equal Employment Opportunity Commission.

- **Axel and Eigil Axgil** (Axel: 1915–2011; Eigil: 1922–1995). Gay. First gay couple in the world to be joined in a registered domestic partnership (Denmark, 1989).

- **Ann Bancroft** (1955–). Lesbian. Adventurer, teacher, author. First woman to reach the North Pole by foot and sled. First woman to cross both the North and South Poles. First woman to ski across Greenland.

- **Deborah Batts** (1947–). Lesbian. First openly LGBT, African-American federal judge.

- **Baron Baden Powell** (1857–1941). Presumed gay. Army officer and writer. Considered the founder of the

International Scouting Movement (Boy Scouts).

- **Laurence Michael Dillon** (1915–1962). Transgender. Physician, aristocrat, and first female-to-male transgender individual to undergo phalloplasty. Author: *Self—A Study in Endocrinology and Ethics.*

In addition, there are many other people who are committed to achieving equality for lesbian, gay, bisexual and transgender people. Here are just a few of them:

FOUNDERS OF NEW ORGANIZATIONS FOR EQUALITY (last 10 years)

- **Juan and Ken Ahonen-Jover** (eQualityGiving)

- **Tico Almeida** (Freedom to Work)

- **Wayne Besen** (Truth Wins Out)

- **Dana Beyer and Sharon Brackett** (Gender Rights Maryland)

- **David Brock** (EqualityMatters)

- **Linda Bush** (Movement Advancement Project)

- **Mitchell Gold and Jimmy Creech** (Faith in America)

- **Georg Ketelhohn and Heddy Pena + 12 more** (Florida Together)

- **Carolyn Laub** (Gay Straight Alliance Network)

- **Robyn McGeehe and Kip Williams** (GetEqual)

- **Dan Savage** (It Gets Better)

- **Josh Seefried and Ty Walrod** (OutServe, which is merging with SLDN)

- **Chuck Williams** (The Williams Institute)

- **Shane Windmeyer, Chad Wilson,** and **Sarah Holmes** (Campus Pride)

HEADS OF MAJOR NATIONAL ORGANIZATIONS FOR EQUALITY

- **Michael Adams** (Services and Advocacy for LGBT Elders, SAGE)

- **Aaron Belkin** (Palm Center)

- **Eliza Byard** (Gay Lesbian & Straight Education Network, GLSEN)

- **Rea Carey** (The Task Force)

- **Kevin Cathcart** (Lambda Legal)

- **Jennifer Chrisler** (Family Equality Council)

- **Clarke Cooper** (Log Cabin Republicans, LCR)

- **Jerame Davis** (National Stonewall Democrats, NSD)

- **Masen Davis** (Transgender Law Center)

- **James Esseks** (American Civil Liberties Union LGBT Project)

- **Herndon Graddick** (GLAAD)

- **Chad Griffin** (Human Rights Campaign, HRC)

- **Jody Huckaby** (Parents, Families and Friends of Lesbians and Gays, PFLAG)

- **Rebecca Isaacs** (Equality Federation)

- **Mara Keisling** (National Center for Transgender Equality, NCTE)

- **Kate Kendell** (National Center for Lesbian Rights, NCLR)

- **Sharon Lettman-Hicks** (National Black Justice Coalition, NBJC)

- **Abbe Land** (The Trevor Project)

- **Ricci Levy** (Woodhull Sexual Freedom Alliance)

- **Aubrey Sarvis** (Servicemembers Legal Defense Network, SLDN)

- **Peggy Shorey** (Pride at Work)

- **Terry Stone** (CenterLink)

- **Lee Swislow** (Gay & Lesbian Advocates & Defenders, GLAD)

- **Rachel Tiven** (Immigration Equality)

- **Adam Umboefer** (American Foundation for Equal Rights, AFER)

- **Chuck Wolfe** (Victory Fund)

- **Evan Wolfson** (Freedom to Marry)

ACTIVISTS AND DONORS WHO ARE MAKING A DIFFERENCE

- **Henry van Ameringen,** strategic donor
- **Ron Ansin,** strategic donor
- **Chip Arndt,** activist and *Amazing Race* winner
- **John Bare,** activist donor
- **Jarrett Barrios,** strategist
- **Vic Basile,** strategist
- **Ignatius Bau,** strategist
- **Dana Beyer,** transgender activist and political candidate
- **Adam Bink,** grassroots activist
- **Brian Bond,** White House liaison
- **Mary Bonauto,** legal ace
- **Marsha Botzer,** transgender activist
- **Jeff Campagna,** activist
- **Tom Carpenter,** strategist

- **Mandy Carter,** activist and Nobel Prize nominee
- **Jerry Chasen,** activist donor
- **Dan Choi,** DADT and equality activist
- **Bobby Clark,** online activist
- **Kate Clinton,** comedian
- **Michael Coe,** communicator
- **Matt Coles,** legal strategist
- **David da Silva Cornell,** activist
- **Anna Curren,** repeal DADT donor
- **Erin Drinkwater,** activist and doer
- **Stephen Driscoll,** democratic activist
- **Liebe and Seth Gadinsky,** allied donors
- **Brian Gaither,** activist
- **Chris Gates,** activist
- **Ethan Geto,** communications strategist
- **Don George,** activist donor
- **Lila Gracey,** strategist
- **Joe Falk,** political donor
- **J Todd "Tif" Fernandez,** grassroots activist
- **Matt Foreman,** strategist
- **Nathaniel Frank,** author
- **Stephen Handwerk,** Democratic activist
- **Craig Harwood,** donor and producer
- **Yashar Hedayat,** strategic donor
- **Stephen Herbits,** strategic doer, and donor
- **Joanne Herman,** transgender educator
- **Daniel Hernandez,** helping hand
- **Kelly Rivera Hart,** Latino and bi activist
- **Steve Hildebrand,** strategist
- **Donald Hitchcock,** strategist and activist
- **Ernest Hopkins,** activist
- **Bob Horvath,** political activist
- **Lane Hudson,** communications strategist
- **Kathy James,** family advocate
- **Brian Johnson,** activist
- **Corey Johnson,** activist and political candidate
- **Hans Johnson,** activist
- **Michael Kenny,** strategist and connector
- **Norm Kent,** publisher
- **Jon Kislak,** allied donor
- **Geoff Kors,** activist donor
- **Lisa Kove,** Department of Defense activist
- **Michael Krawitz,** strategic donor

- **Janice Langbehn,** activist and 2011 US presidential Citizens medal recipient
- **Andrew Lane,** foundation executive director
- **Jeff Lewy,** activist donor
- **Kerry Lobel,** strategist
- **Bill Lyons,** donor advisor
- **Barbara McCullough-Jones,** activist
- **Stuart Milk,** international activist
- **Richard Milstein,** donor
- **Shannon Price Minter,** transgender legal ace
- **Ineke Mushovic,** strategist
- **Kathryn Natale and Janet McLeod,** strategic donors
- **Christopher Neff,** journalist and publisher
- **Richard Noble,** walking activist
- **Derek Newton,** allied campaign strategist
- **CJ Ortuno,** activist ally
- **Dixon Osburn,** strategist
- **Kathy Padilla,** transgender activist
- **Catherine Pino** and **Ingrid Duran,** strategists
- **Libby Post,** communicator
- **Bruce Presley,** donor and producer
- **Lisa Polyak,** marriage activist
- **Donna Red Wing,** strategist
- **Cathy Renna,** communications expert
- **Alix Ritchie and Marty Davis,** agitators
- **Laura Ricketts**, strategic donor
- **Cindy Rizzo,** human sexuality activist
- **Charles Robbins,** youth advocate
- **Mike Rogers,** blogger and citizen reporter
- **Charlie Rounds** and **Mark Hiemenz,** maverick donors
- **Hilary Rosen,** strategist
- **Marty Rouse,** grassroots activist
- **Caitlin Ryan,** family advocate and researcher
- **Rebecca Salokar,** professor and strategist
- **Diego Sanchez,** transgender activist
- **Marsha Scott,** donor strategist
- **Eugene Sepulveda,** donor
- **Garry Shay,** Democratic activist
- **Joel Silberman,** media strategist
- **Howard Simon,** allied defender
- **Maryann Simpson,** donor
- **Barbra "Babs" Casbar Siperstein,** political compromiser
- **Richard Socarides,** activist

- **Palm Spaulding,** blogger
- **Rick Stafford,** Democratic activist
- **Anne Stanback,** marriage activist
- **Mark Steinberg** and **Dennis Edwards,** donors
- **Jim Stork,** strategist and donor
- **Sean Strub,** HIV activist
- **Andrew Sullivan,** author
- **Andy Szekeres,** fundraiser
- **Maxim Thorne,** strategist
- **Lisa Turner,** strategist
- **Urvashi Vaid,** author and strategist
- **Leoni Walker,** donor
- **Jillian Weiss,** transgender activist
- **Bernard Whitman,** communications expert
- **Sara Whitman,** activist donor
- **Jon Winkleman,** political activist
- **Bob Witeck,** communications expert
- **Paul Yandura,** donor strategist and revolutionary
- **Rich Yurko,** activist

APPENDIX 2:

The Dallas Principles

Below is the full text of the Dallas Principles (available at TheDallasPrinciples.org).

It is composed of: Preamble, Principles, Full Civil Rights Goals, and Call to Action. The list of authors follows.

PREAMBLE

President Obama and Congress pledged to lead America in a new direction that included civil rights for lesbian, gay, bisexual and transgender Americans. We now sit at a great moment in our history that inspires the nation to return to its highest ideals and greatest promise. We face a historic opportunity to obtain our full civil rights; this is the moment for change. No delay. No excuses.

Nearly forty years ago, a diverse group of lesbian, gay, bisexual, and transgender people stood up to injustice at the Stonewall Inn in New York City. In doing so, they submitted themselves to bodily harm and criminal prosecution. Their demand was simple—equal protection under the law.

Still today, full civil rights has eluded the same community that rioted forty years ago. Instead, untold sums of resources have been spent to divide our nation and turn our lives into a political football.

At several junctures in American history, the stars have aligned to deliver the promise of equal protection under the law to those previously denied. At this unique time in history, our nation must once again exercise the great tradition of making its people equal.

Justice has too long been delayed. A clear path toward full civil equality for the LGBT community is overdue and must come now.

Using fear and misunderstanding to justify discrimination is no longer acceptable in this nation. Those content with the way things are will be judged harshly by history. Those who do not actively advance these ideals or offer excuses will be judged just as harshly. Those who attempt to divide our community or to delay and deny action on civil equality, waiting for the right moment to arrive, will be held accountable.

We reject the idea that honoring the founding principles of our country is controversial. We believe in the inherent human dignity of all people. No longer will we submit our children, our family, our friends, and ourselves as a political tool for any Party or ideology. A new day has arrived.

PRINCIPLES

The following eight guiding principles underlie our call to action. In order to achieve full civil rights now, we avow:

1. Full civil rights for lesbian, gay, bisexual and transgender individuals must be enacted now. Delay and excuses are no longer acceptable.

2. We will not leave any part of our community behind.

3. Separate is never equal.

4. Religious beliefs are not a basis upon which to affirm or deny civil rights.

5. The establishment and guardianship of full civil rights is a non-partisan issue.

6. Individual involvement and grassroots action are paramount to success and must be encouraged.

7. Success is measured by the civil rights we all achieve, not by words, access or money raised.

8. Those who seek our support are expected to commit to these principles.

FULL CIVIL RIGHTS GOALS

Being united by common principles and engaging in united action, we will achieve the following goals:

1. DIGNITY AND EQUALITY. Every lesbian, gay, bisexual, and transgender person has inherent dignity and worth, and has the right to live free of discrimination and harassment.

2. FAMILY. Every LGBT person has the right to a family without legal barriers to immigration, civil marriage, or raising children.

3. ECONOMIC OPPORTUNITY. Every LGBT person has the right to economic opportunity free from discrimination in employment, public housing, accommodation, public facilities, credit, and federally funded programs and activities.

4. EDUCATION. Every LGBT child and youth has the right to an education that is affirming, inclusive, and free from bullying.

5. NATIONAL SECURITY. Every LGBT person should have the opportunity to serve our

country openly and equally in our military and foreign service.

6. CRIME. Every LGBT person should enjoy life protected against bias crimes.

7. HEALTHCARE. Every person should have access to affordable, high quality,

8. and culturally competent healthcare without discrimination.

CALL TO ACTION

1. We demand that government officials act now to achieve full civil rights without delay.

2. Our organizations and individuals need to develop a collaborative and revolutionary new organizing model that mobilizes millions of supporters through emerging web and phone technologies.

3. All LGBT individuals must accept personal responsibility to do everything within their power for equality and should get involved in the movement by volunteering, giving and being out.

4. We will hold elected officials and our organizations accountable for being transparent and achieving full civil rights by active participation when possible and active opposition when necessary.

5. Our allies need to be proactive in public support for full civil rights.

6. Every government measure that quantifies the US citizenry must permit LGBT individuals to self-identify and be counted in every way citizens are counted.

7. We demand that the media present LGBT lives in fair, accurate, and objective ways that neither include nor give credence to unsubstantiated, discriminatory claims and opinions.

AUTHORS

Here are the authors of The Dallas Principles with their affiliation at the time that the Principles were written.

- **Dr. Juan Ahonen-Jover.** Co-founder of eQualityGiving.

- **Dr. Ken Ahonen-Jover.** Co-founder of eQualityGiving.

- **John Bare.** Activist donor.

- **Senator Jarrett Barrios.** Former Massachusetts legislator.

- **Dr. Dana Beyer.** Transgender and political activist.

- **Jeff Campagna, Esq.** Attorney and LGBT fundraiser and organizer.

- **Mandy Carter.** Nobel Peace Prize nominee and lesbian activist.

- **Michael Coe.** One of the "Most Influential Washingtonians under the age of 40."

- **Rev. Jimmy Creech.** Straight ally working to end religion-based bigotry.

- **Allison Duncan.** Donor advisor.

- **Ambassador Michael Guest.** Senior Advisor to the Council for Global Equality.

- **Joanne Herman.** Donor and transgender rights advocate.

- **Donald Hitchcock.** Activist and former executive director, Gay and Lesbian Leadership Council.

- **Lane Hudson.** Political activist. One of the "Most Influential Gay People in America."

- **Charles Merrill.** Philanthropist (Merrill-Lynch family), activist, and artist.

- **Dixon Osburn, Esq.** Co-founder, former executive director, Servicemembers Legal Defense Network.

- **Lisa Polyak.** Lead plaintiff in litigation to obtain marriage equality in Maryland.

- **Babs Casbar Siperstein.** Transgender activist and board member.

- **Pam Spaulding.** Editor and publisher, PamsHouseBlend.com

- **Andy Szekeres.** Political campaigns consultant and manager.

- **Lisa Turner.** Political consultant and donor advisor.

- **Jon Winkleman.** Political activist.

- **Paul Yandura.** Political strategist and donor advisor.

APPENDIX 3:

Good Companies

Listed below by industry are the companies with a 100 percent rating in the Corporate Equality Index compiled in 2012 by the Human Rights Campaign (www.hrc.org/cei). Note that this list is not exhaustive since there might be companies with a 100 percent rating that have not reported to the Human Rights Campaign:

ADVERTISING AND MARKETING
No companies in this industry reporting 100% rating

AEROSPACE AND DEFENSE
- Lockheed Martin
- Raytheon

AIRLINES
- AMR Corp. (American Airlines)
- United Continental Holdings

APPAREL, FASHION, TEXTILES, DEPARTMENT STORES
- Levi Strauss & Co.
- Nike

AUTOMOTIVE
- Chrysler
- Ford
- Toyota

BANKING AND FINANCIAL SERVICES
- American Express
- Ameriprise Financial
- Bank of America
- Bank of New York Mellon
- Barclays
- Bankcorp
- Capital One

- Charles Schwab
- Citigroup
- Credit Suisse USA
- Deutsche Bank
- Freddie Mac
- Goldman Sachs
- JP Morgan Chase
- Morgan Stanley
- Northern Trust
- TD Bank
- Teachers Insurance & Annuity Association
- Toyota Financial Services
- US Bancorp
- UBS
- Wells Fargo

CHEMICALS AND BIOTECHNOLOGY
- Dow Chemical
- E.I. du Pont
- Genentech

COMPUTER AND DATA SERVICES
- ADP
- EMC
- Hewlett-Packard

COMPUTER HARDWARE AND OFFICE EQUIPMENT
- Apple
- Cisco
- Dell
- Tech Data Corp.
- Xerox

COMPUTER SOFTWARE
- Intuit
- Microsoft
- Oracle
- Symantec

CONSULTING AND BUSINESS SERVICES
- A.T. Keamey
- Accenture
- Aon
- Bain & Co.

- Booz Allen Hamilton
- Boston Consulting Group
- Deloitte
- Ernst & Young
- IBM
- KPMG
- Marsh & McLennan Companies
- McKinsey & Co.
- Navigant Consulting
- PricewaterhouseCoopers

EDUCATION AND CHILD CARE
No companies in this industry reporting 100 percent rating

ENERGY AND UTILITIES
- Exelon
- PG&E
- Sempra
- Southern California Edison

ENGINEERING AND CONSTRUCTION
No companies in this industry reporting 100 percent rating

ENTERTAINMENT AND ELECTRONIC MEDIA
- Time Warner
- Walt Disney

FOOD, BEVERAGES AND GROCERIES
- Brown-Forman
- Campbell Soup
- Cargill
- Coca-Cola
- Delhaize America
- DIageo North America
- General Mills
- Kellogg
- Kraft Foods
- MillerCoors
- Sodexo
- Supervalu

FOREST AND PAPER PRODUCTS
No companies in this industry reporting 100 percent rating

HEALTHCARE / HEALTH INSURANCE
- Aetna
- Blue Cross Blue Shield of Florida
- Blue Cross Blue Shield of Minnesota
- Cardinal Health
- Group Health Cooperative
- UnitedHealth Group

HEALTHCARE / MEDICAL FACILITIES
No companies in this industry reporting 100 percent rating

HIGH-TECH / PHOTO / SCIENCE EQUIPMENT
- Eastman Kodak
- Medtronic

HOME FURNISHING
- Mitchell Gold + Bob Williams

HOTELS, RESORTS AND CASINOS
- Caesars Entertainment
- Choice Hotels International
- Hyatt Hotels
- Kimpton Hotel & Restaurant Group
- Starwood Hotels & Resorts

INSURANCE
- AAA Northern California, Nevada & Utah Insurance Exchange
- Chubb
- ING North America Insurance
- MedLife
- Nationwide
- Prudential Financial
- Sun Life Financial (U.S.)

INTERNET SERVICES AND RETAILING
- eBay
- Google
- Yahoo!

LAW FIRMS
Fifty-five law firms report a 100 percent rating

MAIL AND FREIGHT DELIVERY
- UPS

MANUFACTURING
- Corning
- Cummins
- Herman Miller
- Owens Corning
- United Technologies
- Whirlpool

MINING AND METALS
- Alcoa

MISCELLANEOUS
- 3M

OIL AND GAS
- Chevron

PHARMACEUTICALS
- Bristol-Myers Squibb
- Eli Lilly
- GlaxoSmithKline
- Johnson & Johnson
- Pfizer

PUBLISHING AND PRINTING
No companies in this industry reporting 100 percent rating

REAL ESTATE, RESIDENTIAL
No companies in this industry reporting 100 percent rating

RETAIL AND CONSUMER PRODUCTS
- Abercrombie & Fitch
- Avon
- Barnes & Noble
- Best Buy
- Clorox
- Gap
- Limited Brands
- Nordstrom
- Office Depot
- Replacements

- Sears
- Staples
- TJX
- Uniliver

TOBACCO
No companies in this industry reporting 100 percent rating

TELECOMMUNICATIONS
- Alcatel-Lucent
- AT&T
- Sprint

TRANSPORTATION AND TRAVEL
- Orbitz

WASTE MANAGEMENT
No companies in this industry reporting 100 percent rating

www.ingramcontent.com/pod-product-compliance
Lightning Source LLC
Chambersburg PA
CBHW072357290526
45794CB00001B/94